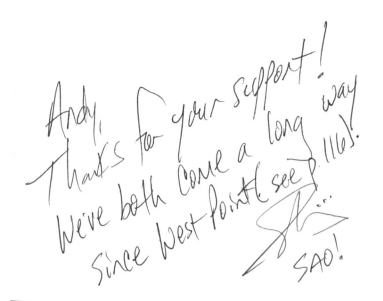

Andy,
Thanks for your support!
We've both come a long way
since West Point (see p. 116)!
SAO!

SON OF A SOLDIER

eddie williams

*Success is not a snapshot of where you are
but measured by the obstacles you've overcome*

SON OF A SOLDIER

success is not a snapshot of where you are
but measured by the obstacles you've overcome

For more information, contact E & M Williams Consulting Group LLC, 1720 Mars Hill Road, Suite 8151, Acworth, GA 30101, 770-356-1562 or eddiewilliams49@gmail.com.

This book includes information from many sources and personal experiences. It is intended to be used as a guide and a resource for its readers. The publisher and author do not claim any responsibility or liability, directly or indirectly, for information or advice presented. While the publisher and author have made every effort to ensure the accuracy and completeness of the material, we claim no responsibility for potential inaccuracies, omissions, incompleteness, error, or inconsistencies.

Front and Back Cover design: Kevin Heffner
Author photo: Kevin Heffner
Layout design: Tudor Meier
WCG logo design: Jeffrey Stone
Back cover family photo: Jamie Bogner
ISBN: 978-0-9897633-0-1
Library of Congress Control Number: 2013914721
Printed and bound in the United States of America.

ACKNOWLEDGEMENTS

Thanks to those who have been prodding me for several years to both tell my story and put it on paper for others to read; Dave Weber, Thom Suddreth, Michelle Suddreth, Kevin Heffner, Becky Spain, Jill Phillips, and Ynes Rosas.

I want to also thank all the people who have been an influence to me and assisted with my many drafts, providing edits, revisions and candid feedback; Mike Pniewski, Lee Martin, Jimmy Starnes, Earnest Davis, Sam Peng, LynnMarie Earl, Mike Wien, Dr. Tim Morrison, Michael Berg, Carlos Greene, Chris Hill, Denny Collins, Bill Hicks, Rob Collins, Suzanna Savoie, Larry Martens, Joseph Bartlett, Dan York, Stacy Zwijacz, Michael Tinsley, Dale Hartsfield, David Bignault, Michael Page, Dan Branham, Bill Pamplin, Dennis Hooper, Tony and Cathy Bagdonis, and Dez Thornton.

I especially want to thank the United States Military Academy, West Point Class of 1981. Our class motto, *Strength As One*, so aptly reflects how we supported and encouraged one another through those tough four years between R-day and graduation. We've continued to support one another throughout our respective military and civilian careers.

A heartfelt thanks to my Infantry and Special Forces (Green Beret) brothers, particularly those on ODA-036 and ODA-011. You are the most elite soldiers in the world. It was my pleasure to serve alongside you.

DEDICATION

This book is dedicated to my parents, Foster and Lilli Williams. You modeled love and courage under extremely difficult circumstances throughout your lives and marriage together. To my brother, Tommy, who continually challenged me and often protected me as we grew up.

It is also dedicated to my wonderful wife Maria Williams, and our strong, loved, and self-confident children, Evan and Madison. Thanks for your support and encouragement to get this book completed. I'm sure my constantly open laptop was annoying, as I continuously edited and revised the manuscript. You knew how important it was for me to write my story and share it.

I love you with all my heart.

Son of A Soldier is an exciting and impressive undertaking. Eddie's personal story, military experience, and civilian career are appropriate extensions of his business endeavors. It makes perfect sense to connect his book to his speaking and lecturing programs. In a real sense his book serves as a take-away for his corporate audiences, as well as, for the academic community, youth groups, and next generation adults, who can benefit from his been-there-done-that analysis and tribute on success.

Colonel Peter Dillon, Retired
Former Commander,
7th Special Forces Group

Son of A Soldier is a winner! Eddie's multi-cultural heritage that resulted from being bullied is a story that will resonate with many. His achievements speak for themselves and his story needs to be shared with a broad audience.

Dr. Dwight "Ike" Reighard
President/CEO MUST Ministries
Senior Pastor Piedmont Church

Son of A Soldier *is not only touching but educational and inspiring as well! It is awesome!*

Chaplain (COL) Tim Ridley
Command Chaplain
Headquarters
Georgia State Guard
Clay National Guard Center
Joint Force Headquarters

Eddie's story is intriguing, well-written and extremely passionate. A personal catharsis. It is not only a testimony of Eddie's love, honor and respect for his parents, who had everything to do with his success, but it allows him to lay out very real pangs he experienced in life, and uncover family secrets hidden for so many years."

Lee Martin
Vietnam Veteran, Retired Colonel
Author of; *Provocation,*
The Third Moon Is Blue, and
The Six Mile Inn

TABLE OF CONTENTS

W hen I was walking between classes one day in high school, an African-American girl stopped me in the hallway. She looked at me and bluntly asked, *"What are you?"* Surprised by her question, I could only assume she was asking me about my ethnicity or race. I confidently replied, *"I'm black!"* Without hesitation and with a voice so loud I'm sure all the other students around us could hear, she responded, *"YOU ARE A LIE!"* Shocked by her words and bluntness, I felt humiliated and tried my best to regain my composure and quickly walked away. Embarrassed, I escaped by melting back into the flow of students and got to my next class before the bell rang.

Everyone, me included, has stories of their embarrassments, failures, accomplishments and successes. My life has been filled with a variety, and many were worse than the awkward school hallway encounter. I heard countless hate-filled epithets, got dagger-like stares, and faced humiliating situations from both strangers and even people I knew. Frankly, all of those people were just plain nasty and rude.

We've all been positively and negatively influenced by people throughout our lives. Some helped us overcome obstacles, recover from stumbles, and encouraged us toward achieving our destiny. They were family, friends, co-workers or colleagues— individuals who mentored, prodded, and even pushed us toward our goals. They set a foundation upon which we then applied our respective strengths, talents, gifts, and abilities. Yet, on our road to maturity, we've also gotten misdirected, drifted off course, or found ourselves outside our comfort zone. How we overcame those obstacles and uncomfortable situations along the way, depended so much on what we'd learned from those in our lives who helped us stay focused. Because they gave us a hand up when we were knocked down, it is critically important that we acknowledge those who positively influenced us to overcome uncomfortable moments and awkward events. For me, two of those influential people were my parents. They were the source of my motivation and the inspiration for my future adventures, even though I didn't realize their full impact on my life until after they were gone.

My parents passed away just a few years ago. As the executor of their estate I had the extremely tough task of clearing out my childhood home and sorting through their personal papers, photos, and documents. Anyone who has ever had to do this can probably relate with me. This daunting task brought with it a flood of memories. As I sorted through my parent's things, I discovered that they saved many of my childhood items: birthday cards, school projects, report cards, and other memories. Finding these items was emotionally tough because of the sentiments they brought back. I also found numerous legal documents, certificates, and family papers. My task was made even worse when I uncovered several family secrets.

I wrote this book because of what I discovered about my family—and in the process learned about myself. I learned how my parents overcame many challenges and obstacles during their youth and throughout their marriage. I also learned much about their strength and character while simultaneously gaining clarity about my family history. My parents imparted much to me during my youth, which directly influenced how I handled my own challenges and hurdles. They seasoned me with confidence, self-esteem, focus, and the mental toughness to reach my own goals, overcome obstacles, and share insights with others.

My story will help you! For some, it will be a brief glimpse into America's traumatic history—merely a generation ago. For others, it will be an opportunity to acknowledge your own challenges, prompt a journey of reflection to uncover your mentors, or maybe launch a discovery of your family history. Be forewarned, you'll probably uncover family secrets in the process. This book is my story. Yet, it will inspire you to take action to research and ask questions to uncover yours. When you do, acknowledge those who helped you learn and grow. Then be willing to share that knowledge.

—*Eddie Williams*
August 2013

"Nothing is really ours until we share it."

~*C. S. Lewis*

CHAPTER 1

The Batcha

"Ability is what you're capable of doing.
Motivation determines what you do.
Attitude determines how well you do it".

~ **Lou Holtz**

Many years ago, when I was nine years old, an event occurred that is still indelibly imprinted in my memory. When my older brother and I misbehaved our mom took the needed actions. She was the main disciplinarian in our home and had the full-time job of managing our family. My dad served in the military and usually left for work early in the morning—well before I got up for school—and returned home around dinnertime or later. When I got into trouble my mom took action with one of her cleaning tools. Her tool of choice was originally designed to hit and air-out our bed comforters. We called it the *batcha*. About four feet long and made from woven bamboo, it had a flat webbed paddle at one end. I distinctly remember a critical aspect about the *batcha*. It hurt!

My mom had a slender frame and stood about five feet seven inches tall. She was also very smart. She wouldn't always use the *batcha* immediately after I'd done something to deserve it, nor would she chase me or my brother around the house with it. Sometimes she'd wait for an opportune time when I least expected her wrath. She was known to wait a few hours or even days later, before she'd find the right moment to move close, then reach out and ... *whack!* Out of the blue she'd surprise me with it, taking two or three swings to reinforce her displeasure. There were times when I'd thought I'd gotten away with a misdeed, and knew it was a waste of my breath to ask her why she unexpectedly swung at me with the *batcha*.

On that particular day, I'd left dirty clothes on my bedroom floor instead of putting them in the laundry hamper. Later that afternoon while watching TV, out of the corner of my eye, I saw Mom approach with the *batcha* in her hand. I'd faced this opponent before and knew what was coming. Just as she set her swing in motion I ducked out of her reach. She missed. Score one for me. That was the good news. At that moment, I'd had enough of being hit with that thing and made up my mind that I didn't want to feel its sting ever again. Before my mom could take a second swing, I grabbed it, jerked it out of her hand and tossed it aside. I then turned toward her, our eyes met, and I said defiantly, *"Mom, you aren't going to hit me with the batcha anymore!"* I felt triumphant! Metaphorically, the bell rang signaling the end of the bout. Although taking a stand to avoid the *batcha* that day was a significant moment in my childhood, the rest of that day's events proved to be an even greater milestone for me.

Maybe you can remember a significant moment like this during your own childhood? An event etched in your memory regardless of how long ago it had occurred. A turning point when your rebellious spirit bubbled up and you took a stand for your own individuality or independence. It may have been when you aced a difficult test, got your driver's license, or evaded a neighbor's angry dog while stealing fruit from their backyard tree. You can reflect back on that event in your life because it proved to be profound. Yet, maybe it was a disappointing event; such as a bad blind date, a fumble during a football game against a hometown rival, that first car accident, or striking out in the bottom of the ninth inning with a runner on third. Those events were victories and disappointments of our youth and had timeless significance.

Eddie versus the *batcha* was one such moment for me. At the instant I took it from my mom, I'd achieved a personal victory and expressed self-confidence. I'd demonstrated defiance, grit, and chutzpa. I'd also reached a new stage of youthful maturity. Athletes call it *cockiness*, *raising the bar*, or *elevating to the next level*. Yet, when this happens, it's typically accompanied by that quiet voice in the back of our minds telling us that we've crossed the line—the thin line that separates self-confidence and stupidity. Often, during our youth, we don't realize when that line has been crossed until it's too late. This was precisely the situation between my mom and me that day.

The very act of celebrating my triumph affirmed in me some fundamental youthful belief. I'd won. At the end of the bout, having enough sense to put some distance between us, I confidently went outside to play. However, I was too young to fully realize that the bout was not over. We'd only concluded the first round. There were consequences for my actions because I'd crossed that thin line.

As I think back to that day, I should have realized something even more important had occurred—much bigger than just defeating the *batcha*. It was more about my mom's demeanor following my defiance. She'd displayed something about herself in a very subtle, yet significant way. My mother didn't get mad or follow me outside. She didn't even yell at me. For some reason, my actions and rude comment didn't seem to bother her at all. I'm sure she didn't expect my behavior and tone, but she just stood there and watched me walk away. I also recall the expression on her face; that uniquely parental facial expression which simply says, *"You are in so much trouble!"*

It's an expression any parent can instantly display toward a child, especially when that child has done something wrong or said something inappropriate. On that day I'd done both! Can't you picture that *look* on your parents' faces? No words are exchanged, just that unmistakable expression you'd seen so often. Maybe it was a teacher, a grandparent, or other relative who could instantly display their *look* of displeasure; the glare in their eyes or frown on their forehead that spoke volumes. Though my mom had her *look*, maybe your parents spoke to you in a specific tone of voice or called you by your full name—which signified that you were in big trouble.

Today, as a parent myself, I can still recall my mom's facial expression on that day so long ago. The memory still gives me chills. If you were to ask my own children they would tell you that my wife and I each have our own unique *look* that we've displayed toward them. A *look* that either stops them before acting on an impulse, or makes them think twice before doing or saying something they shouldn't. It's the *look* that has sometimes said, *"I am so disappointed in your behavior"* without uttering a single word.

It wasn't until years after the *batcha* incident that I fully realized the true source of my mom's *look* and why she displayed such calmness that day. Her stoic manner came from the depth of her character and a lifetime of experiences, not merely because of her displeasure with my defiant words or actions. As a child I didn't always understand the rationale for my parents' behavior. Only after they passed away and I sorted through their belongings did

I fully appreciate them. I discovered several significant realities about them and why they acted, or didn't act, in certain ways. To explain what I mean, let me rewind the clock back to a time several years before my seemingly victorious *batcha* moment.

Below is a statement I found in my parents' papers. It's from a U.S. Army letter written early in my dad's military career:

> *I, Lieutenant Frank C. Drake, Commanding Officer of Specialist Four Foster Williams, do hereby grant my permission for him to marry Lilli Waldmann, a German National, at the American Embassy located in Basel, Switzerland.*
>
> **~Dated June 15, 1962**

Yes, you read the words correctly. Amazing as this may seem today, a U.S. Army Officer, the commander of my dad's military unit, had to give my father permission to marry my mother. To shed more light on this specific circumstance, here is another document I uncovered among my parent's files:

ZIVILSTANDSAMT
DES KANTONS BASEL-STADT

Telephon (061) 24 38 50
Domhof Basel

Basel, am June 26th, 1962

```
         S t a t e m e n t
         -----------------
```

We, the undersigned, Foster Williams, Citizen of the United
States of America, of Alexandria (Louisiana), and Lilli
Waldmann, of German nationality, declare as follows :

We know that after the Law of the State of Louisiana,
of which the groom is a resident, the marriage between
members of the Negro and the Caucasian race is not allowed
and absolutely void.

We know therefore, that this marriage, performed to-day,
XX June 26th, 1962, will be void in the said State of
Louisiana.

This marriage will be performed on our own responsibility
and we shall discharge the Swiss Authorities and the Zivilstandsamt Basel from all responsibility.

Declared and signed before the civil marriage ceremony on
Tuesday, June 26th, 1962.

Basel, June 26th, 1962

When these documents were written, my dad was a soldier in the
U.S. Army and stationed in Germany, where my mom lived. My
parents were married in Basel, Switzerland; a politically neutral
country to the laws of America and Germany. The wording
of these documents and the fact that they were both written
in 1962 are significant, because they reveal details about my
parents' situation and their character. They are also historically
important because this was around the time of America's Civil
Rights Movement.

20

The U.S. Army has had tens of thousands of soldiers stationed in Germany since World War II, and the U.S. Government established certain accommodations. One of the many U.S. Army policies was if a soldier wanted to marry a German national, the soldier was required to get permission from their commanding officer. Adding to the sensitivity of my parent's situation, my father was black and my mother was white.

Today, mixed-race or bi-racial marriages are commonly accepted in America. Yet, only a generation ago they were very uncommon, and in many states illegal—especially in the South. Louisiana was one of them. That was why in 1962 my parents had to travel to Switzerland to get married. They had to both abide by U.S. Army policy, and then travel to a neutral country, so they wouldn't violate United States law. Clearly, these papers show my parents' determination to do whatever they had to do in order to legally become husband and wife. Frankly, I didn't know that either of these documents existed until after they passed away.

Dad during his early career in the U.S. Army

As I read and sorted through their documents, I reflected on the tremendous strength they both displayed throughout their lives together. I'm humbled when I think back at their personal determination to marry and raise a family—while enduring what must have been an unbelievable amount of racial abuse, verbal torment, humiliation, and personal discomfort. All of this was compounded by their respective physical pain and health issues.

My mother lost her courageous battle to ovarian cancer in 1997. For most of her life, she also suffered from severe rheumatoid arthritis and other ailments. Her hands and feet became progressively and severely deformed due to this debilitating joint illness. She often asked me to open jars or packages of food, button her jackets and coats, give her medicine, and help with numerous other daily tasks she couldn't do herself. Despite her crippled hands and feet she kept an immaculately clean house. You could literally eat off the kitchen floor and see your reflection on each appliance. Every plate, pot, pan, and glass was spotless and in its proper place in her kitchen. She constantly cleaned our house. We owned a washing machine but not a dryer. Though she had limited use of her hands, my mom still used clothespins to dry laundry on clothes-lines in our backyard. She was a very proud homemaker and wanted every guest to feel comfortable and welcome in our home. She would instantly prepare a full meal for anyone who dropped by.

My father also suffered from several ailments and illnesses. He had diabetes, high blood pressure, dementia, and chronic back problems because of his military service. He wouldn't let any of those conditions prevent him from being a devoted husband, father, soldier, and proud man. I remember his first job after retiring from the military. He worked at a furniture store loading heavy items into delivery trucks—despite his bad back. He was determined to provide for his family. He died from a combination of his medical conditions and a heart attack in 2005.

As a kid I didn't realize their strength of character, partly because I was too young, too naïve, and partly because my parents chose to shield me from their hardships as best they could. Only now, just a few years after they passed away, can I truly appreciate them. Looking back with the benefit of maturity, clarity, and several discoveries in their personal items, I can now better understand and appreciate events that I personally witnessed. Frankly, many of those events occurred at a time when I was unable to fully grasp their significance. Now, so many years later, they've become clear. I'll do my best in the coming pages to share many of those stark events, recollections, family secrets, and how they directly impacted my life. First, let's finish the story of my perceived victory over the *batcha*.

The bad news following my incident with my mom occurred when my father came home from work later that night, she told him what I'd done and said. I was in bed pretending to sleep, but could hear their conversation just outside my bedroom door. Within seconds my father burst into my bedroom, scooped me up with one hand, and held me tight so I couldn't wiggle away. With his other hand, he took the military belt from around his waist and wore out my backside. With each swing he explained why I'd made a bad decision when I took the *batcha* from my mom. He also pointed out that my defiant comment to her was neither appropriate nor appreciated, and my misbehavior was

Mom with baby Eddie

never to be repeated. His words were direct and to the point. My dad didn't curse, but left no room for misunderstanding. His displeasure with my actions earlier that day was very clear. Though I'd avoided the pain of my mother's swings, I later felt the greater pain of my dad's belt. Clearly, that was not the victory I'd counted on.

Thinking back on that day's events, I can now smile and even laugh about them. I remember not being able to sit comfortably for a day or two because my backside was so sore. Though I didn't realize it at the time, I'd actually glimpsed at a snapshot of my parents' character and gained some important life lessons. Obviously, one was to never again take the *batcha* from my mom. In fact, after that day, when she'd hit me with it—even when it didn't hurt anymore—I'd cry or complain as though it did. I preferred the *batcha* over my dad's belt.

Several other teachable moments came from that day. Each was much more significant than just accepting my parents' discipline. My parents demonstrated to me something critical in their behavior—especially my mom's calmness. She had an almost serene reaction to my rebelliousness. I'd gotten a peek at her inner strength by her reaction. Recall, after I grabbed the *batcha* she didn't seem flustered, ruffled, or surprised. I should have taken a cue from her reaction—or non-reaction—but I was too young to recognize the significance of her composure. I'm sure she knew that my dad would come home later that night and help handle the situation I'd caused. Understandably, my dad's actions to my behavior were typical. Yet there was an underlying significance about his demeanor too. His reaction was much deeper than just the correction he'd given me. He wanted to teach me some lessons, even if I was too young to understand them. Clearly he wanted to teach me not to act impulsively, to be more respectful to my mother, and that there were consequences for my actions. But it wasn't until years later that I fully understood, comprehended, and appreciated the more critical lessons he wanted me to acquire that day.

CHAPTER 2

Being Bullied

*"Our chief want is someone who will inspire us
to be what we know we could be."*
~Ralph Waldo Emerson

W hen I was walking between classes one day in high school, an African-American girl stopped me in the hallway. She looked at me and bluntly asked, *"What are you?"* Surprised by her question, I could only assume she was asking me about my ethnicity or race. I confidently replied, *"I'm black!"* Without hesitation and with a voice so loud I'm sure all the other students around us could hear, she responded, *"YOU ARE A LIE!"* Shocked by her words and bluntness, I felt humiliated and tried my best to regain my composure and quickly walked away. Embarrassed, I escaped by melting back into the flow of students and got to my next class before the bell rang.

As harsh as my situation seemed, we've all had embarrassing moments because of the words or actions of people we've encountered. What's critically important about them is how we responded to those experiences. Are we shocked at the harshness of their words or the evil in their hearts? Do we retaliate in like manner to those critics whose sole purpose in life seems to be to aggravate, upset, humiliate, or degrade us? Like a stiff wind, they want to send us off course, knock us down, or distract us from our journey. They live for the pleasure of stealing our thunder and diminishing our self-esteem. They don't want us to have any peace and joy. What, then, is the appropriate response we should have toward them?

A critical lesson my parents modeled for me when I was growing up, is when dealing with people like this, I didn't have to respond to their criticism, bullying or torment. Often, our best response is no response at all. Though this might be difficult to do, don't let other people's jeers, taunts, or snide comments impact us. Here's why! Sooner or later, we will all encounter people who just aren't going to accept us, work with us, or even like us. For me, one was the girl who embarrassed me in the high school hallway so many years ago. We will meet people—who out of their own ignorance—won't accept us because they don't know us or care to know us. To her, I was a student with a light complexion and she didn't understand why. She was a skeptic. She either didn't want to know why or simply didn't care. After my reply, she immediately and bluntly discounted my answer.

Maybe my high school hallway situation reminded you of similar events in your own past. Those embarrassing moments brought back by looking at old school photos, your yearbook, or when a family member says *remember when you were …* moments. Only after reflection did their significance become clear, like the common phrase *hindsight is 20-20*. Sometimes reflecting on our past brings clarity to why things occurred in a certain way and how those events impacted us.

One of my moments was the unexpected challenge by the *"You are a lie!"* statement. It was a light-bulb moment. When we've said to ourselves, *"Oh, now I understand why that happened?"* We all know how critical it was to fit-in during our high school years. Until the hallway encounter, I had never had my ethnicity or blackness questioned, especially not in such an in-your-face manner. The girl had openly and loudly called me out about my race. Was it that hard for her to figure out my race? Why was it even an issue? I had no idea! But, at that instant it was unbelievably embarrassing to be publicly questioned by her. I was shocked by her words and tone. Rather than stay there, I had to gather my composure and escape. Walking away was my best, immediate and only option. Avoiding any further embarrassment simply made sense. Yet, looking back I can only ask myself, *why did I act that way?* Maybe my reaction was sub-conscious. My fight-or-flight response had kicked in. I now realize that my reaction was actually very conscious. Growing up I'd seen my parents react this way in situations that were much worse. I instinctively knew that this was how I also needed to react. At that moment, it was my turn to do what my parents had modeled for me hundreds of times before.

While I was growing up, I didn't fully understand the significance of all that my parents tried to impress on me. Yet after I became an adult, many of my own interactions, even personal achievements, were firmly rooted in what they had instilled in me and modeled for me. Maybe it's the same for you. Haven't you occasionally thought back to your own youth, in order to gain clarity on why events played out the way they did. Why certain things happened or didn't happen? Those reflections might even reveal why you act more like your mom or more like your dad. They explain why you're stubborn or timid, avoid conflicts, purposely miss family reunions, or constantly fill the role of mediator with your siblings.

Life provides us with a broad playing field to experience challenges, learn things, achieve victories, and overcome adversities. There are also those times when we are reluctant to get in over-our-heads. Those circumstances and unexpected events in our lives when we're uncomfortable, even threatened. When we fear the unknown and have no control. However, it's exactly then when we should demonstrate our own personal grit and judgment. Our reaction is what allows us to continuously learn and grow toward achieving our personal, individual or professional successes. What's crucial is how we apply the knowledge gained from those critical times, life lessons, or teachable moments. It's how we handle those circumstances in our lives—whether unusual crises or everyday difficulties—that improve our self-awareness. When we're knocked down do we get back up, dust ourselves off and move on? When we're publically embarrassed, do we stay and argue or move along to minimize the damage? Often, we must do what is extremely difficult for us human beings to do—ignore them. We need to acknowledge those awkward moments, yet learn from them. We should also learn to celebrate the thrill of our victories along the way. Only then can we appreciate the journey and the impact of our mentors. We should also minimize those negative people—the naysayers, skeptics, and critics, who always seem to be in our lives.

The Williams family when I was a little kid

Here's what I mean. We won't always succeed at everything we attempt. We will all experience some sort of setbacks during our lifetime. Some are the result of events or caused by other people.

But the critical question during those times is—how will we handle them? Equally important, how will we handle the critics? Those people who seem to place hurdles in our path. They enjoy reminding us of our failures, stumbles, and flaws. Some chastise us simply because we are different. How should we respond? What is our natural reaction? Our first gut response may be to respond in kind, to return ill will for ill will, to lower ourselves to the same level of spite with which we've been treated. Frankly, we have the options to either reply to their spitefulness or not. The first approach has rarely proven successful. We have probably all seen for ourselves, how those situations could grow worse. Nothing good would have happened if I had debated my *blackness* with the girl in the hallway. The other option was to ignore a bad situation and choose simply not to react. This option was the toughest to do. We have to talk ourselves into a gracious attitude, merciful response, or just walk away.

To emphasize this point, let me ask a simple question. Were you ever bullied in school? The U.S. National Institutes of Health provides a sobering statistic that 75% of students are bullied. Maybe you were picked on because of the clothes you wore, or because you were taller or shorter than other students. Maybe they belittled you because you ran faster, jumped higher, or were a better athlete. Perhaps you were the target of harsh and demeaning words because you had red hair, freckles, or big ears. Maybe someone didn't like your skin color. This caused you to be the target of their bitterness, resentment and even their ignorance.

In his book, *Sticks and Stones Exposed*, author Dave Weber cites research by a professor of anthropology, describing evidence of extreme abuse. Dr. W. Penn Handwerker links depression, suicide, stress, and heart disease as a result of the actions of others. A stark example was the aggression witnessed in the

1999 Littleton, Colorado public school shooting. At Columbine High School, twelve high school students and one teacher were shot and killed by two teen students. They resented and acted out because of the hurtful words of fellow students. Handwerker's research discusses the impact of belittling and demeaning behavior, treating someone as inferior, and attempting to make people feel bad about themselves.[1] Handwerker's research disproves the children's riddle, *sticks and stones may break my bones, but words will never hurt me.* Handwerker validated that words hurt and the effects last a lifetime.

We need only watch the local or national news to see examples of schoolyard bullying and the toll it takes on our youth. Cyber bullying has also become a critical national issue. Bullying through the use of the Internet, text messaging and twitter are quite common among today's youth. Unfortunately, several teens have taken their own lives because of the verbal abuse and comments they've experienced from peers and fellow teens. As a result, school systems across the country have established policies to crack-down on the various forms of bullying. Several entertainment figures, celebrities, pop and rap music artists, and athletes regularly produce anti-bullying ads, public service announcements and marketing campaigns. Visit any school and you'll find anti-bullying posters, 1-800-help lines, and numerous Internet support group links prominently displayed in school hallways and on websites.

Sadly, some of us grew up with parents, siblings, or other family members who belittled and demeaned us since childhood. We were convenient targets for their caustic comments. Maybe they didn't succeed at something in their own past and took out their failures or frustrations on family members—especially vulnerable ones. As a grown and responsible adult, you may still have an older brother or sister who treats you as if you are still ten years old and don't know anything about anything. Those people seem to hang on to their own bitterness, nurse their resentment and even cultivate it at your expense! They continually take it out on us as if they were doing us a favor. The mental and verbal punishment they inflict on us somehow brings them joy and their own type of misplaced justice. They still find opportunities to target us for their demeaning words like; *"You're never going to amount to anything."* or *"You're a loser!"* They want their bitterness to eat away at us. They try to steal our joy. This is such a pitiful human tendency. It has even permeated the venues beyond the schoolyard and home. Workplace bullying is well documented in business articles and case studies.

As a child of mixed-race parents, I was bullied in the school hallway. I must not have been *black enough* for the girl who stopped and questioned me. Frankly, within the African-American community, there is a serious issue between light-skinned and dark-skinned black people. The term *colorism* has evolved that divides skin complexion within the black community. This issue is such a silly and meaningless one. Yet it's something I've had to constantly deal with.

Growing up, I wasn't white so many of the white kids—or more accurately their parents—didn't let me hang out with them. The black kids who didn't see me as *black enough* didn't want me to hang out with them either. I was often called names like, *mulatto* and *half-breed* (partly because of a song by the then-popular singer Cher, which was frequently played by radio stations). Thanks, Cher! I was shunned by classmates whose parents didn't want me to be friends with their children. Several fathers didn't want me dating their daughters or even hang out with them. When I went to their homes, their parents didn't let me in or didn't want to meet me. They only let their daughters talk with me while they stood inside the open doorways. Those situations made me mad.

I was a good kid and was being treated this way for something I had no control over—my skin color. Those situations were just plain embarrassing and I couldn't do anything about them. But, I also wasn't going to let them demoralize me.

I grew up during the 1960s and 70s. This was an especially turbulent time of emotional and racial tensions at the height of America's civil rights movement. My parents, my brother and I were often the targets of nasty words, epithets, and demeaning taunts because we were a bi-racial family. My parents helped me overcome those experiences, even when I didn't fully understand why people acted the way they did toward us. My parents both demonstrated and modeled for me appropriate reactions during those times. They simply did not respond to other people's taunts and nasty comments. When we ate at restaurants my parents ignored the stares, pointed fingers, and just-loud-enough-for-us-to-hear whispers from other patrons. I'd learned from my parents that often the best response was not to respond at all. When I asked my dad why people acted this way toward us, he told me that their behavior showed their ignorance. They were unwilling to accept us because of our skin color. I'm sure my dad could have given me a much more in-depth explanation, but I believe he wanted me to have his best age appropriate answer. At the time it made sense to me.

Though my parents did their best to shield my brother and me from abuse, I now realize why we didn't drive to certain parts of town or shop at certain grocery and department stores. I eventually understood why they thought it best to avoid the potential encounter or verbal abuse. But they couldn't completely protect us from every situation or rude comments. There were several times when I saw, heard, and witnessed the abuse. I often heard the *N-word* directed at me or my family when we shopped or ate out. At other times I heard the *"N... lover"* term directed at my mom while we were in public places. My parents had to continually encourage me to ignore them. Growing up,

My parents celebrating at a New Year's Eve party

I constantly observed how my parents dealt with these incidents. As simplistic as this sounds, they taught me that those and other harsh words were from people who simply *didn't know better*. As I look back on those times, I am amazed how they maintained a stoic and positive attitude during those disturbing moments.

I also understand why my parents were direct when they disciplined my brother and me. Their discipline was not only to correct our misdeeds or misbehavior. It also demonstrated how to have a reasoned response. They wanted to teach us not to over-react to situations, but to react appropriately. And more importantly, they taught me to think before reacting. They encouraged me to learn from my mistakes and not continue behavior that would lead to even more serious consequences. My mother's calmness during her times of tension and surprise was her way of modeling for me proper behavior during tough times. Recall, that during the *batcha* episode her *non-reaction* was her reaction and my dad's behavior was an appropriate but *measured* reaction.

My dad was strong and stoic in most any situation. He rarely got angry or raised his voice. In fact, when my brother and I would yell or scream at one another, my dad would intercede using one of his favorite techniques to stop our feud. He would firmly— and loud enough so we could hear him over our yelling—say just a single word, *"please"*. He wanted us to please settle down. Please stop arguing. Please work out whatever the disagreement was about. It didn't always resolve the problem between my brother and me, but it often redirected our energy, even if only to separate us or have us stop and think. It brought attention to our feud. My dad's technique made us pause just long enough to consider other alternatives. We'd either decide to settle our disagreement, realize that further yelling was worthless or simply separate and do something else with our time.

Though my dad had his flaws, I also learned some important lessons about how he dealt with them. He was extremely afraid of heights. I once witnessed this fear on a family trip driving through the Sierra-Nevada mountain range between northern California and Reno, Nevada. The highway curved so sharply that you could see the steep drop-off merely inches from the roadway. About halfway up the mountain road my dad became so paralyzed by the height and danger that he pulled off at a rest area. He told us that he couldn't drive any further. My mom couldn't drive because of her crippled hands and feet. After a brief conversation with my mother he gathered himself, pulled our car back on the road, and kept his eyes fixed on the back of the car in front of us. All along the twists and turns to Reno, he was encouraged by my mother's calming voice, continually telling him, *"you're OK honey ... we're going to make it just fine. We'll be there soon"*.

My dad never learned to swim and was afraid of water. Nevertheless, he often drove us to a spa in Calistoga, California, about an hour from our home. It offered natural hot springs treatment and hot water pools to help relieve my mom's arthritis and ease her painful joints. My dad would wade waist deep into the pool and encourage her as she slowly swam laps.

These, and so many other events, reinforced my parents love and support for one another. They were just a few of the many ways I recall how they provided mutual encouragement to get through their trials and obstacles. I learned much about them by seeing their interactions and discovered even more in reading through their personal documents. They each had tough upbringings.

My dad grew up near Lake Charles, Louisiana. Though he rarely talked about his childhood, he did tell me that his parents died when he was a young boy. On some of the military papers that I found, where it required information about family history, he'd written *parents deceased—unknown reason*. He and his sisters were raised by their grandparents on a farm in Bunkie, Louisiana. My dad once told me that he hated overalls, because they were practically all he wore growing up. At the outbreak of WWII he joined the U.S. Army to help in the war effort and to get off the farm. He also served in the Korean War. He seldom talked about his military service. Only after I pestered him to find a picture of him in uniform, would he grudgingly tell me about what he did in the wars. I enjoyed those times when he shared a few wonderful nuggets with me. In WWII, he served in an all-black Quartermaster (supply) and Transportation unit that supported the military campaign in England, Africa, Italy and Germany. In fact, one of the units he served in was designated as the 1936th Quartermaster Truck Company (Aviation) (Colored).

Specialist Foster Williams serving in Germany

Note: It's worth mentioning here that this was a time of conflict within the military regarding integrated colored (Negro) and white soldiers. Here are the first few paragraphs of an in-depth analysis and study of integrating soldiers that was formally written by the U.S. Army's Chief of Military History.[2]

The principle problem in the employment of Negro Americans as soldiers in World War II was that the civilian backgrounds of Negroes made them generally less well prepared than white Americans to become soldiers or leaders of men. This problem was greatly complicated by contemporary attitudes and practices in American society that tended further to inhibit the most efficient use of Negroes in military service. Despite these handicaps Negro soldiers played a larger role in the most recent Great War than in any previous American conflict. While the bulk of the more than half a million of them who were overseas by early 1945 were serving in supply and construction units, many were directly engaged with the enemy on the ground and in the air. If proportionately fewer Negroes became combat troops than the Army had contemplated in its prewar mobilization plans, this was true for white soldiers as well. Global war generated a need for service troops far greater than anyone visualized before Pearl Harbor, as well as a need to use all able-bodied Americans regardless of color or other distinction in military or civilian support of the war effort.

The integration of whites and Negroes in the armed forces of the United States in the early 1950's and the continued rapid advance of Negroes in the American economic and social order have substantially altered the circumstances governing their use as soldiers a quarter century ago. Nevertheless another full mobilization of American manpower for national defense would again bring to the fore many of the problems described in this volume.

Washington, D. C.
18 June 1965

HAL C. PATTISON
Brigadier General, U. S. A.
Chief of Military History

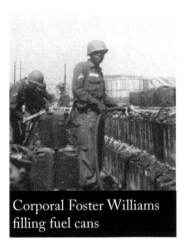

Corporal Foster Williams filling fuel cans

My dad served as a truck driver and moved equipment, food, fuel, bombs and ammunition where needed to support America's war effort. Lifting, loading and unloading heavy boxes and containers caused him to later have back problems. After twenty-six years of service he retired with partial disability.

My mother grew up in Germany and was a young girl during the rise of the Nazi regime. Like many Germans, she and her family never joined the Nazi party, but still endured the activities that raged throughout their country. Like my dad, my mom rarely mentioned the details of her youth during that turbulent time. Candidly, I think she was embarrassed about what Germany had become under the tyrannical Nazi regime of her childhood. In those brief moments when she did, they were harsh memories. My mother and her family were victims of WWII. Her parents died in the war. Her mother was killed in their family home during a bombing raid in 1943. Her father ran a butcher shop in their small Bavarian town. He was killed in it during a separate bombing raid in 1945. On both occasions, my mom and her older sister had to identify their parent's body. As young women at the time, they supported one another after their parents were killed. In the years following WWII, both married American soldiers and put the terrible tragedies of the war behind them. Among the things I found in my parent's safe deposit box, were both of my maternal grandparents' birth and death certificates, a few of my mom's childhood photos, jewelry I'm sure belonged to her mother, and the family Bible.

After all they had experienced, I'm amazed how my parents displayed and maintained a wonderful attitude about life. Only now, as I look back on my own childhood, do I realize the many positive attributes they modeled for me. I witnessed how they responded to offensive people, who called them nasty names and even spat at them. In so many uncomfortable situations, my parents displayed much about their character. When they could have easily—and justifiably—responded harshly or in the same way that people had treated them, they chose to display the opposite. They demonstrated a wonderfully positive attitude. In fact, I recently came across a very well written piece by Charles Swindoll, who appropriately defines the attitude my parents so often exemplified;

Attitude

The longer I live, the more I realize the impact of attitude on life. Attitude, to me, is more important than facts. It is more important than the past, than education, than money, than circumstances, than failures, than successes, than what other people think or say or do. It is more important than appearance, giftedness or skill. It will make or break a company...a church...a home. The remarkable thing is we have a choice every day regarding the attitude we will embrace for that day. We cannot change our past... we cannot change the fact that people will act in a certain way. We cannot change the inevitable. The only thing we can do is play on the one string we have, and that is our attitude...I am convinced that life is 10% what happens to me and 90% how I react to it. And so it is with you...we are in charge of our attitudes. [3]

~ Charles R. Swindoll

CHAPTER 3

From Coal to Diamond

"We are what we repeatedly do.
Excellence, then, is not an act, but a habit."

~ Aristotle

Throughout our lives we are constantly influenced by people. Sometimes those encounters are incredibly positive, while at other times they are decidedly negative. Yet, the attitude we display during each of those encounters is our choice. We have the choice to either let someone's words or actions upset us, or we can minimize—even ignore—the impact. If we choose to react, it's also our choice to what extent we do so and how we handle the consequences.

To clarify what I mean let me ask a question. How does a chunk of coal turn into a priceless diamond? The answer is—constant pressure endured by the coal over a long period of time. Pressure exerted on the coal actually molds it into a rough and jagged stone. After the rough stone is shaped and polished by a skilled jeweler, it is transformed into a stunning diamond. Similarly, the difficulties, tough times, and pressures we face during our lives will result in us being shaped and molded into our destiny. We mature into our potential and vision for our lives. The key is how we endure and react to our respective pressures. This ultimately results in how we realize our opportunities—many of which we could never have imagined.

Okay, I can hear you responding, *"Eddie, are you telling me that I just need to put up with other people's pressure and abuse, and the opportunities will eventually happen? Really! But, you don't understand my situation. You don't know what I'm dealing with! You aren't walking in my shoes."* You're right! I don't know your situation. I don't know the details of your pressures, the people you're dealing with, or what you're enduring. Clearly, I hope you are in situations where you have the choice **NOT** to let other people's words or actions affect you. But that's not reality. When they do, remind yourself that you have the choice to overlook, or even ignore their words and actions. If possible, remove yourself—either physically or emotionally—from the situation. If that is not possible, remember that you have the choice about how to react to their comments, rudeness, and pressures. Oftentimes, my parents didn't have that choice. They could not avoid the rude and nasty comments directed at them. They just had to endure them and then make conscious choices about how to react—or not react.

Like my parents, you may not have the ability to remove yourself from uncomfortable confrontations. You can't just walk away from the harsh words directed at you from someone in your home or workplace. The hurtful and intimidating words hurled at you might even come from your boss, your co-workers, or even your spouse. Clearly, it's not easily possible to avoid situations that occur when family members or work colleagues throw negative barbs your way. You can't just leave your house—though a good walk outside might be appropriate to cool things down after a heated confrontation. Consider how many times you have been the focus of harsh comments with no way to avoid them. I hope you have the option to seek the advice and help of professional counselors, mediators, or clergy. I hope that you have ways to escape those encounters.

Let me share another childhood incident to help illustrate this point. One day, I was so mad at my parents because they didn't allow me to play outside with my friends that I ran away from home. Now that I have my own kids, I fully realize that my parents were looking out for my welfare and safety. They also knew that I wasn't feeling well that day, and that bad weather was quickly approaching. As a kid, I didn't know or care about the reasons I couldn't go outside. That didn't matter to me. I wanted to play with my friends. As I snuck out of my house, I remember thinking to myself, *"I'll show them! I'll just stay away so they'll miss me and realize that they should have let me go outside anyway."* I'd only gotten a few blocks down the street, when I was startled by the sounds of the approaching thunderstorm. Looking for someplace to hide, I crouched behind a clump of bushes in a neighbor's front yard. Soon the rashness of my actions became even more evident when a pair of the largest and meanest looking dogs came trotting up to me. They sniffed and barked at me for what seemed like an eternity. I was scared and certain I was about to become their lunch. At that instant, I realized my mistake to run away. As soon as the dog's owner called them away from my hiding place, I headed straight back to my house. *Whew!* I was so glad to be back in the safety in my bedroom and actually welcomed the scolding from my parents.

What's my point? Whether as adults or children, I believe that we all have had similar experiences when we haven't rationally or logically thought things through. We've impulsively acted out or spoken out about something and it got us into trouble.

In hindsight, those were revealing moments of poor judgment, from which we have hopefully learned important lessons. Those times are *teachable moments* that develop our maturity. As a child, my defiant attitude and poor judgment got me a scolding and almost bitten by scary dogs. As adults, acting impulsively can get us into much more serious trouble. Obviously, our challenges are not as simple as a child running away from home, barking dogs, or approaching thunderstorms. Our challenges are much more intense situations in our homes or workplaces. They could be differences of opinion between work teams, or opposing views with management about the best way to handle a project, a problem, or a business issue. Maybe our challenges are personality differences between co-workers due to a lack of effective communication. Steven Covey, the famous inspirational speaker and author summarizes this neatly in his popular book, *The 7 Habits of Highly Effective People*, *"Seek first to understand, before seeking to be understood."* Covey promotes the importance of communication because *"most people do not listen with the intent to understand, they listen with the intent to reply. They're either speaking or preparing to speak. They're filtering everything through their own paradigms [filters]"*. He emphasizes that effective listening is so powerful because, *"it gives you accurate data to work with. Instead of projecting your own autobiography and assuming thoughts, feelings, motives, and interpretation, you're dealing with the reality inside another person's head and heart. You're listening to understand. You're focused on receiving the deep communication of another human soul."* [4]

The concept of seeking to understand is critical as we daily face difficulties, setbacks, disappointments, failures and challenges in our lives. As we go through inevitable disappointments or tough times—and even feel as though we're being buried by them—we may fail to understanding the outcome that they will have on us. Like coal, we're sometimes under pressure in a dark and lonely place. But we also need to recognize that we're being molded by that pressure. Pondering and meditating on it—rather than the end result—only drains us of valuable energy. My family felt that way when we heard rude comments and racial slurs from the many people who couldn't accept us. My parents didn't focus on other people's negativity (the pressure) but on how their own lives were evolving and what the outcome would be some day. They certainly could have been negatively affected by the weight of the constant abuse they encountered throughout their marriage. But they didn't let others' ridicule deter them from their goals. They were married for nearly forty years. They had very productive lives and raised two confident, smart, and responsible children in the process. Instead of being buried by insults, harsh words, and distasteful comments, they remained strong and steadfast. They also continuously supported and encouraged one another. They didn't let the tough times and injustices derail them. They wanted to enjoy their marriage together, raise a family, and model for my brother and me how to appropriately handle the pressure we were sure to experience.

I learned to stay true to the direction they set for my future. At nine years old, I'd rejoiced at the brief success and victory over my mother's discipline, only to be brought back to reality by

Dad on the job at Ft. Meade MD

my father's response. My apparent *batcha* victory was not the correct focus. It was just a single step toward learning the bigger lessons my parents were teaching me. As a result of my reflections on the events of that day, so many years ago, I gained greater wisdom about my parents and the foundation they had provided me.

While you may have already achieved some personal or professional successes, along the way you've probably also had disappointments. Maybe your life hasn't turned out the way you'd planned. The reasons are many. You were mistreated. You didn't have the resources. You didn't stay focused. As a result, maybe you've given up on your dreams. You let people or the situation derail you and just settled in for the long haul. I contend that the plan for your life shouldn't go away just because you've had disappointments or setbacks. Don't write off your goals just because you've made some bad decisions, mistakes, or the result of someone's negative impact on you.

If it provides some comfort, realize that other people have made some of the same mistakes as you. Some have even made those really huge *whopper* mistakes. Take solace that you can get past and overcome those setbacks. Here's how! Don't focus on the setbacks. They will only drain you of the energy to learn, recover, grow, and move forward. View all of them as bumps along the road to more success. I challenge you to persevere toward achieving your goals and regain control of your hopes and dreams. Reset your goals, re-boot your vision, and re-establish your objectives so that the path still ahead will be the best part of your life! Continue to believe in yourself and set a course for your success. It will be an amazing journey not just for you, but for those you care about and those you will positively impact along the way.

Chris Gardner, author of the #1 New York Times Bestselling memoir, *The Pursuit of Happyness*, inspired many through his story of overcoming obstacles. He transformed himself from homelessness to wealthy stockbroker. His book was produced into a very successful movie of the same name that starred actor Will Smith. In his second book, *Start Where You Are; Life Lessons in Getting from Where You Are to Where You Want to Be*, Gardner writes, *"If you've just had the rug pulled out from under you and your loved ones, whether you're facing the loss of a home, a job, or dealing with a health or financial crisis, hope and help from those who've survived the worst and gone on to thrive are here to encourage you."* [5]

In other words, how you allow others to help you handle your adversities says a lot about you and makes a huge impact on your success. When facing difficulties, if you shrink back, or choose to be bitter about your dilemmas, you are allowing them to get the better of you. When you lose your enthusiasm, you're letting the hardship keep you from your dreams. If you choose to keep pressing forward—especially with the help of positive mentors and role models—you'll continue to rejoice even during hard times. You are actually allowing your true character to emerge. Having this perspective, allows you to set yourself up for promotion to the next level of success in your life. Inspirational speaker and author Stephen Covey puts it this way:

> *"As we make and keep commitments, even small commitments, we begin to establish an inner integrity that gives us the awareness of self-control and the courage and strength to accept more of the responsibility for our own lives. By making and keeping promises to ourselves and others little by little, our honor becomes greater than our moods. The power to make and keep commitments to ourselves is the essence of developing the basic habits of effectiveness. Knowledge, skill, and desire are all within our control."* [6]

Well defined and written goals allow each of us to value our work, our talents, our gifts, and our contributions to the greater good. They impact our effectiveness to our family, our bosses, our co-workers, our friends and most importantly—ourselves. It was exactly that way for my parents, despite the negativity they encountered. They had plans for their future, a greater good for their lives together, and a positive impact on my brother and me.

CHAPTER 4

Hit the Target

"A ship that has not set its course,
finds no wind favorable."

~ **Socrates**

My parents did not have to get married, especially during the turbulent environment that we now know was America's Civil Rights movement. As a mixed-race couple it was a certainty they would encounter uncomfortable situations and deal with difficult people. Knowing this, they did not obsess about everyone's reactions. They could have played the *"what if"* mind game; *What if something goes wrong? What if they got in trouble? What if their marriage wasn't recognized? What if they got arrested?* The *"what if's"* could have been overwhelming and endless. The odds were against them. Recall, mixed-race marriages were not widely accepted or even legal in several American states including my dad's home state of Louisiana. That was why they got married in the neutral country of Switzerland. Even so, they knew that they would flatly not be accepted by some people. Despite that, they also chose to have children. Why would they want their children to experience similar abuse or discomfort? My parents wanted to press forward with their dreams. They wouldn't let their bi-racial situation and the certain discomfort they would face in America, deter them from living their lives together and raise a family. Together they traveled down the road of life, enduring its many bumps, twists, turns, forks, and potholes along the way.

I'm confident that my parents had a strong conviction that they would eventually be accepted. They refused to let ignorant people intimidate them or let circumstances restrict them. They didn't conform to others expectations, cultural constraints, or a host of other influences. My parents were confident that they would overcome adversity, while instilling in my brother and me the qualities of self-confidence and self-esteem. With this strong and secure foundation, my brother and I also would overcome our own exposure to people's taunts, jeers, cruelty, and ignorance. My parents believed that they would be able to handle the racial discomfort they would experience, and was certain to come for their children.

My Mom, Dad and me during a fun moment at home

Let me encourage you to have that same conviction when you encounter discomfort. Everyone will have their own share of difficulties and bumpy roads. Those roads are filled with tragedy, financial disaster, and bad choices. We can anticipate some of the twists and turns we'll encounter along those roads. Others will pop up without much warning catching us off guard and may even be life-threatening. If the plans along your road didn't work out the way you wanted, it doesn't mean your journey wasn't worth the effort. The dead end alley may have taken you somewhere you needed to go at the time. There will be times when you must dig your heels in and hold fast to fulfilling the promises in your heart. Also, don't assume that if something has worked for you in the past, it's going to continue to work out for you in the future. In other words, don't get so set in your ways that you avoid trying new things or taking new paths. Be open to change. I've heard it said, *"nothing is as constant as change."* I believe that this is an essential truth. Let me explain this point another way.

Imagine you were watching a major sports event, such as the NFL Super Bowl or the NBA Basketball Finals. Suppose that before the game began, you already knew the outcome. You knew the winning team and the winning score. You knew the final result regardless of how far the winning team fell behind in the early stages of the game. No matter how bad things looked, you didn't yell at any player's mistakes or the referee's bad calls. During the course of the contest, you didn't get irritated or upset at any misstep or flaw. Your emotions didn't change, and you were neither exhilarated nor disappointed from start to finish. Why not? You had inside information. You knew the winning team before the contest even started.

How amazing would it be if this were possible? You had the ability to know the outcome. Now consider if that event was your own life? You knew the exact date and time of major achievements—or failures—well before they actually occurred. The date you would meet your spouse, get your first job, a major health situation, when your children would be born, the death of family members, and the exact date of your retirement. As a result of knowing all of this information beforehand, you'd probably have a peaceful, uncomplicated, content and calm life.

Imagine that you actually had the ability to know all of these critical milestones. Your life was a bulls-eye.

Now, assume that each of those critical events was represented by arrows, and you knew that every one of them was guaranteed to hit your bulls-eye. No missed shots. No arrows would fall short. None hit the ground. None flew off into uncertainty. Each arrow hit the center circle every time. What an amazing journey that would be. I can hear you already saying, *"That's impossible. That can't happen!"*

Alice and the Cheshire Cat

Let me address your response this way. Do you recall reading Lewis Carroll's book, *Alice in Wonderland?* If so, remember during Alice's adventure, she traveled down the road which eventually splits into two paths. Alice reached a fork in the road. There were now two different ways she could continue. Recall, at the fork in the road stood a large tree, with a broadly smiling Cheshire cat seated on a branch.

Alice and the Cheshire cat had a simple yet profound conversation:

Alice: Which road should I take?
Cheshire cat: Well that depends on where you want to go.
Alice: I really don't care!
Cheshire cat: Then it really doesn't matter which road you take, does it? [7]

The Cheshire cat's remark to Alice, "*Then it really doesn't matter which road you take, does it?*" is a very insightful statement. The Cheshire cat is sharing with Alice that since she doesn't have a clue about her destination, it matters little which road she takes. Obviously, we don't have the luxury of knowing the winning team before the game is played. Likewise, we don't know all of the twists and turns that life will take before they occur. Unlike Alice, we should have goals that give us direction in our own path of life. Goals are important. Without them—and the bulls-eye to aim at—we are simply going down the road of life without any purpose or direction. Without them we won't know which fork in the road to take at any particular time. Some people take any road when they reach a fork because they're not sure which way they should go. They may not even know where they want to go or even how to get there. They are *directionally challenged.* Even with a GPS they get lost. They are subject to whatever happens to them along the way. Have you noticed this in anyone you know?

I propose that we should have our own personal direction, especially when it leads to our personal fulfillment. Obviously, having goals (arrows) and tangible outcomes for our life (bulls-eye) are different for each of us. They might be a large bank account, health for our family, a successful career, no debt, an around-the-world vacation, or many other potential desires. Achieving happiness is different for everyone and we each have our own respective definition of it. I'm not passing judgment on what they are, but simply stressing that goals are critical toward reaching our respective desire for happiness. In fact, I suggest that to better understand something, it often helps to define its opposite. A friend of mine shared with me the following definition of unhappiness; *"not knowing what you want, but working your guts out to get it."* Many people can probably relate to this definition. They may not have well-defined, tangible, and written goals. Recognized business consultant and speaker Brian Tracy puts it this way, *"Fewer than three percent of adults have written goals and plans that they work on every single day. When you sit down and write out your goals, you move yourself into the top 3% of people in our society. And you will soon start to get the same results that they do."* [8] Tracy's comment then, begs the questions; what are the other 97% doing? Are they aimlessly wandering down life's path—like Alice?

We are all at various stages of achieving our goals. You may be a teenager trying to survive school and pass your next pop-quiz or test. You may be a young adult just starting out in your career, or a newlywed couple barely keeping your financial heads above water. You may be a single parent or middle-aged couple with some successes behind you and many more dilemmas in front of you. Perhaps you're surrounded by friends, co-workers, or family members who always seem to get ahead, while you just tread water or feel stuck in quick-sand. Too often, some people believe that if they only made more money, or worked longer hours, they could obtain all of the things others around them seem to so easily possess. But, we also don't always know the specific situations or heavy burdens of those around us. The seemingly well-to-do neighbor who can't sleep at night because of their stress in managing the massive debt they've hidden so well. The successful co-worker in the fancy corner office actually detests their new promotion because of the work load and responsibilities. Don't get fixated on being like others. My parents clearly knew that their mixed-race marriage was unique at the time. They certainly weren't trying to *keep up with the Joneses*. They established their goals and did their best to achieve them.

Let me offer a definition of goal setting: *have a good idea of what you want, what you want to do, and who you want to become.* Whatever your circumstances may be today, stay true to your goals. Your victory in reaching them might happen tomorrow, within the next month, ten years from now, or beyond. Along the way, be confident that the achievement of your goals is in store for you. There will be forks along the road to success that will impact whether you achieve your goals. Also, some of the people you will encounter along the way will try to derail you. Let me encourage you not to listen to their negative and self-defeating comments. The girl in the school hallway was one of those people early in my life. She wanted to steal my self-esteem. People like her only drain energy. Also, don't pay attention to limiting thoughts that may occasionally creep into your mind. It will drain your energy and enthusiasm too. No matter how close or far the achievement of your goals seems to be, no matter how badly things look, take a few seconds to encourage yourself. Have positive self-talk like: *"I don't know why this is happening to me right now, but it's just a matter of time before I'll get through it."* Believe in yourself—and take the time, to believe in yourself. In fact, many very famous and successful people overcame significant failures and had to ignore critics, before achieving their own success. Here are a few:

- **Abraham Lincoln** failed twice in business and was defeated seven times in politics before he was elected president in 1860.

- **Elvis Presley** was fired by the Grand Old Opry in 1954. Some told him to go back to driving a truck.

- **Thomas Edison** tried two thousand experiments before he invented the light bulb.

- **Marilyn Monroe** was told by the Blue Book Modeling Agency in 1944 to give up modeling.

- **Sylvester Stallone's** screenplay was rejected nineteen times before he decided to produce "Rocky" himself.

- **Henry Ford** failed and went broke five times before he finally succeeded in business.

- **Babe Ruth and Hank Aaron** were both known for setting baseball's strike out record. They each also held baseball's home run record during their careers.

- **Robert Frost's** poetry was rejected by the Atlantic Monthly magazine because the editors considered it "too vigorous."

When asked about how he achieved his prestigious major league baseball batting title, Hank Aaron replied:

> *My motto was always to keep swinging. Whether I was in a slump or feeling badly or having trouble off the field, the only thing to do was keep swinging.* [9]
>
> **~Hank Aaron**

You create your own future. You determine the final score of your own contest. You determine what road you will travel down. Even when you encounter bumps or forks along the way, you'll be better because you endured them. You'll feel joy bubbling up on the inside of you again, refreshing you and giving you strength. Unlike Alice, you'll know which path to take when you reach a fork along your road of life. When one path ends, purposefully pick another and confidently travel down it. When one plan doesn't turn out the way you'd like, start another plan. Strive to hit your own personal and professional bulls-eye.

Let me put it another way, *the only difference between a rut and a grave is the depth*. Don't get stuck so deep that you find yourself without alternatives or options. Don't continue to do the same thing, the same way, time after time or year after year. Albert Einstein's popular definition of insanity is *doing things the same way and expecting different results*. Handling change, especially change which produces positive goal-oriented actions, takes deliberate effort.

Essentially, I'm saying that we have to get out of our comfort zone. We all probably know someone who has lost their enthusiasm. They don't have the same zest for life they once had. At every encounter with change—even if that change meant increase or advancement—they shrink back to their comfortable ways of doing things. They might not realize it, but by constantly operating within their comfort zone, they may prevent themselves from getting to the next level of achievement, experience new things, or get closer to reaching their goals. My parents certainly understood this concept. They lived outside of their comfort zone. In 1962 their bi-racial marriage challenged societal norms as a married couple. Their marriage challenged the laws of my dad's home state of Louisiana. Growing up I witnessed many of their encounters and the reactions of those who wouldn't accept our family. Even so, my parents kept their determination to live their lives together and eventually passed along their tenacity onto my brother and me. This was foundational when I had to deal with my choices and challenges, achieve my personal and professional goals, get out of my comfort zone, and deal with inevitable change. It hit me like a ton of bricks.

CHAPTER 5

The Gangs

*"Our doubts are traitors, and make us lose the good
we oft might win by fearing to attempt."*
~ William Shakespeare

As children, we've all been asked the question; *"what do you want to be when you grow up?"* Some of us had no idea how to answer this question. There were so many options and we had no clue about our future profession or vocation. Others may have had a fear of uncertainty or even a fear of failure. Why? Because they didn't believe they would acquire the skills, resources, or tools to achieve success. They may have even had an honest fear of success. The uncertainty of what would happen after graduating from high school or college was a scary prospect. You may know someone with that perspective. They're afraid to learn a new language, software program, how to use Twitter, an iPhone, or fearful to accept a new role at work because of the resulting change it might bring. Their personal self-talk says, *"Oh no ... now what?"*, because the change will put them outside of their comfort zone. They may actually have to learn and apply new skills, meet and lead new people, or manage unfamiliar situations. The resulting change will bring on higher stress levels. Studies show that a negative mindset is an important predictor of how stress affects us. If you believe something is bad for you, it will be. But you'll be happier, healthier, and more effective if you see the difficulties and challenges you face as opportunities to learn and grow, rather than as just a *daily grind*.

We should view stress differently. Reframe it as an opportunity that creates mental toughness, clarity, and self-confidence. Think back to when we first learned how to ride a bike, play a sport, or drive a car. How about when we took up painting, photography, trained for a 10K road race, or attempted numerous other challenges. Some people learn new tasks quickly and easily. Others have difficulty at first, but eventually become comfortable after practice and familiarity. Even others will have little interest or gave up when they can't master new tasks.

I still recall some of my answers to that familiar *"what do you want to do when you grow up"* question. As a little boy I wanted to become a doctor, then a soldier like my dad. As I got older, I wanted to be an astronaut, a police officer, an architect, a kung-fu ninja fighter, a professional football player, and even a race car driver. At any given time, my answer reflected the latest TV show or movie I'd watched or book I'd read. But, it was during my sophomore year in high school, when I needed to begin making some critical decisions about my future. It was then, when my relationship with my parents and their personal situation had a critical impact on me.

Throughout my high school years my parents gave me lots of guidance about the importance of education. They helped me focus on my ambitions, stressed the importance of getting good grades and a high SAT score. They also continuously checked with my teachers on my progress, often attended parent-teacher conferences, and encouraged me to attend college. Maybe you can recall someone who took an interest in your future and ambitions. Maybe it was a parent, older sibling, or someone who provided guidance and was a positive influence. My parents played that key role for me, partly because they wanted me to have a better future than what they'd achieved. Though both completed high school neither graduated from college. The potential of my brother or me doing so was a significant goal for them. They helped me stay focused on my future, even when I had several opportunities in high school to jeopardize it, make life-altering mistakes or take a wrong path.

After my dad retired from the U.S. Army, our family settled in the small town of Richmond, California, on the east side of the San Francisco Bay Area. Richmond was a few miles from the larger cities of Berkeley and Oakland, both known for liberal perspectives, open-mindedness, and *if-it-feels–good–do–it* thinking. Richmond also had a wide assortment of ethnic groups, multiple cultures, and a variety of gangs. Some of them were the Black Panthers, Hare Krishnas, Hippie groups, Asian and Mexican gangs. Two of them were the *Chicanos* and *La Raza*. Several students in my high school were gang members. They actively recruited on campus to bolster their ranks. Rival gangs occasionally had fist or knife fights during school hours. From time to time, the fights even resulted in shootings. I remember a fight during lunch one day when a member of one gang was shot in the back by a rival gang member. A few days later I learned that the bullet hit the victim's spine and permanently paralyzed him from the waist down. Fortunately fights at school were the exception. Most of the time the gangs were smart enough to avoid one another. They limited their interactions to taunts and stare-downs saving their fights for nighttime or weekends.

Though I was approached about joining, being a gang member never seemed to be something I wanted to do. But, I did hang out with a group of classmates. We were just a bunch of high school kids with the common interest of helping each other graduate. We were a diverse assortment of students: a couple of varsity football linemen, two basketball players, a few members of the band, a couple of nerds, geeks, a physically disabled kid, and me. Frankly, we all just wanted to get through high school and avoid trouble. There was safety in our diversity and numbers.

I particularly remember one member of our group. His name was Fred and he was a quadriplegic. I don't recall how he was injured but he rode around our school using a motorized wheelchair. He operated it by tilting a control toggle with slight movements he still had in one of his hands. Everyone seemed to look after Fred. We opened doors for him, helped him get books from his locker, his lunch and snacks, and even pushed his wheelchair over high curbs and doorway thresholds. Fred was always upbeat. He greeted everyone with a friendly smile and thank you. Frankly, I don't ever recall him being depressed about his condition. It would not have surprised me if one day he stood up, got out of his wheelchair, and with a big grin told everyone he really wasn't disabled at all. We all would have laughed along with him as if he'd played a big joke on us. Fred never seemed to let his disability get him down. He had obstacles well beyond what any of us could imagine but he was always upbeat. Candidly, I think that because Fred hung out with our diverse group, the rest of the students, including the gang members, seemed willing to accept us too. In fact, many of the gangs also helped Fred navigate around school. It was the right thing to do. It also helped them gain acceptance.

Most of the students in my high school had a mutual understanding regardless of whether we were gang members, nerds, or just ordinary students. Collectively we were a bunch of kids from different backgrounds, each trying to survive. But each group or gang kept to their respective hang-out areas during class breaks, lunch, and after school. Some clustered on the wooden benches at the ends of each school building. Others hung out in the open courtyard by the band room or in the grassy areas near the various school entrances. We respected one another's turf.

The group I belonged to included kids from different ethnic and cultural backgrounds; black kids, white kids, Asian kids, Italian kids, rich and poor kids. More importantly, no one made a big deal about me being bi-racial. It didn't seem to be an issue within the group. I just fit in. It also helped that my older brother and I attended the same high school for a few years. He was two grade levels ahead of me, stood six feet three inches tall, and unofficially made it known that I was his little brother. He hung out with his own diverse group of classmates. Some of them also had younger brothers or sisters at our school. They informally looked after their siblings and often influenced school behavior.

A couple of those situations involved me. One was an incident in PE (Physical Education) class during my freshman year. We were playing a touch football game on the grass field on the back side of campus. On that day I was the quarterback for my team and threw a long pass to one of my friends and teammates. My pass was a little short and the football hit one of the kids from the other team on the head. He happened to be a member of one of the toughest gangs, was twice my size, and really ticked off at me. After shaking off the impact, he started running toward me with clinched fists. Just before he reached me—and I'm sure with every intention of beating me to a pulp—one of his friends yelled at him saying, *"Don't hit him, he's Tommy's little brother"*. The guy stopped just before running me over. With extreme self-control he only yelled at me to never let that happen again. All I could do was think to myself, "*Whew, I survived!*" With a stammering voice I was barely able to respond, "*OK!*"

A few weeks later, I played catcher during a softball game in PE. The same gang kid from the football incident was again on the opposing team. At one point during the game, he was on third base when one of his friends hit a pop-fly to deep left field. After the ball was caught he tagged-up and headed for home plate at full speed. He barreled over me so hard that I had the wind knocked out of me and was out cold for a few seconds. If the PE Coach hadn't been there, I probably would have taken even more punishment. That's just how it was in my school. Sooner or later there was payback.

Don't misunderstand the relationship between me and my brother. Though we were together at the same high school for a couple of years, we weren't chummy. His presence didn't guarantee my absolute safety. He couldn't always back me up every time I got into a scrape. He and I also had various sibling issues because of our four year age difference. We always seemed to have totally different interests and maturity levels. Though we had a few of the same friends, we rarely hung out together. In fact, when we would pass in school hallways or in the cafeteria we barely acknowledged one another. For as long as I can recall, we've had *brother issues* growing up. Candidly, some of those issues still exist to this day. But that is another story for another book.

Staying in—and ultimately graduating from high school—was important to me and many of my classmates. Getting good grades, or at least good enough to get into college, was our goal. We operated by an unwritten rule that anyone who was willing to help his or her classmates with their school work was left alone. I seemed to be one of those students. The combination of having my parent's encouragement, being a fairly smart kid, and having the ability to make friends easily helped me survive high school.

My parents wanted my brother and me to get a good education in order to get good jobs and become responsible adults. They instilled in me a level of self-confidence that insured my future was not dictated by what other people said or did, but based on my own achievements and determination. One of the things that seemed to especially help me was my ability to easily make friends. This was the result of the many moves our family made while my dad was in the military. When he was transferred from one base to another, I learned to quickly adjust to the new location. As soon as the movers showed up with our furniture, appliances, and household items, I'd immediately look for the boxes labeled *Eddie's room.* Then I'd rip them open, find my baseball glove and baseball, or my football, run outside and announce, *"Hey, I'm Eddie. Anyone want to play catch?"* Within minutes, I was playing catch with three or four new friends. For me the new military base was not just the location for my dad's new Army job. It was another opportunity to make new friends.

Eddie (standing, far left) on the Pee Wee League Baseball Chiefs

I offered to help classmates who struggled in subjects where I was comfortable. We had group study sessions in the library during study hall or at lunch. We'd work on memorizing and practicing our foreign language class skits. My friends also helped me when I struggled with my challenging subjects, pre-calculus and physics. Those who were good at writing reviewed my papers. We'd help one another with pre-test reviews. Again, surviving high school and staying out of trouble was a common theme for most of us. That said, there were plenty of chances in school and also in my neighborhood that could have easily derailed me.

My high school was an inner-city school. The surrounding neighborhoods offered lots of distractions; drugs, alcohol, crime, poverty, broken families, gangs, teen pregnancy and several others. I lived in a rough part of town and from time to time those realities became quite evident. One day I was playing a pick-up baseball game with some buddies in a public park a few blocks from my house. Just as we were finishing up the game, we heard gun shots coming from the other side of the park. We hurried over to see what had happened and saw the lifeless body of a man lying face down in the street. Blood had already pooled around him. The police were talking to witnesses and neighbors about the incident. Apparently, the man had gotten caught in bed with another man's wife. The husband came home earlier than expected and the victim didn't get away fast enough. That was the first time I'd seen a dead body—but not the last.

There was also a routine to the activities in my neighborhood. It was characterized by families looking after one another. Neighbors were attentive to any strange vehicles or unusual events. We checked up on one another, especially the elderly. Some kids in my neighborhood, especially those whose parents were on welfare, got their only balanced meal at school lunch because they were so poor. Those students who were very good athletes (*jocks*) enjoyed special attention and given special *local-kid-does-good* status. Our school's track, baseball, and football teams played their away games all over Northern California. For many those trips were probably the only time they traveled outside the Bay Area. For some those trips provided opportunities to get away from the violence and turmoil within the neighborhood. For others those trips were brief escapes from the dysfunction within their homes. Many families didn't own a car. The local public transportation system called BART (Bay Area Rapid Transit) and city bus service (AC Transit) were their only means of transportation. My family had one car, but my dad needed it to drive to work every day. Walking or taking the city bus was normal for most of us. I either took two city busses or walked to school with a bunch of friends. It was a treat when one of my buddies with a car, would see me at the bus stop and offer to drive me the rest of the way. When I walked, the trip was about forty minutes and allowed us to talk about stuff; like girls, school activities or weekend plans.

If I wore my rented tuxedo to school I got it free for the prom

Though life in my neighborhood was tough, neighbor looked after neighbor. We picked up the newspapers and mail when someone was out of town. We were quick to notice a strange car or any activity that seemed out of the ordinary, especially since this was well before organized community watch programs. We prepared meals when someone was sick or in the hospital. Parents wouldn't hesitate to call one another if their child hadn't returned home when expected. We'd welcome a new family to the neighborhood by bringing over a covered dish or cake. My mom loved baking BUNDT cakes for a new neighbor.

I also remember that everyone looked after each other's kids. My parents looked after my friends when they came over, and their parents looked after me when I was at their house. If I was at a friend's house around lunchtime or dinnertime, it was common to become part of their family meal and vice-versa. Parents commonly called one another to get approval. Adding another plate to the kitchen table was no big deal. Frankly, I was introduced to many cultural foods while at my friend's homes. It was also quite common to get corrected by any adult when you misbehaved. When you did something wrong while away from home, you hoped that the adult who'd corrected you didn't know or call your parents. If they did, you got punished or scolded again when you got home.

On weekends, my friends and I were often gone all day playing everything from pick-up football, basketball, or riding our bikes all over the East Bay hills. We often rode ten or even twenty miles away from home most every weekend. My parents had no clue where I was. The typical curfew was to be home by dinnertime on school nights, or when the street lights came on during weekends. Even then, we could still play after dark, so long as we were within shouting distance when our moms called us home. I could hear my mom's voice for blocks.

School provided us numerous social activities. Alongside the formal student body hierarchy (Class President, Vice President, etc.), there was also an informal student hierarchy. We supported and encouraged the jocks. We had a couple of really athletic students who were scouted by the local and state colleges. I remember a kid named Eddie Miller, who was one of the most talented football running backs and basketball point guards within our local East Bay high schools. A family of brothers; the Nicks brothers were very competitive multi-sport stars. Each excelled at track, basketball, football, and baseball. I especially remember in the class ahead of mine, there was an extremely talented and versatile multi-sport athlete named, Willie McGee. He was an extremely good baseball player. A few years after I graduated, I heard his name mentioned in the national sports news. After college, he was drafted by the St. Louis Cardinals baseball team. Willie McGee was named that year's Major League Baseball Rookie of the Year and had a long and storied career.

For students who were not exceptionally athletic, like me, there were several other avenues for us to fit in. We had several extracurricular organizations; such as, the National Honor Society, language clubs, various science clubs, the yearbook club, the student band, and many others. For me, those clubs helped me socialize, build more friendships, and served as support groups. I joined the National Honor Society and the German Club. Our German language teacher was a Japanese-American lady, who we called Frau Takeda. She majored in German in college and was a gifted teacher. She also mentored many of her students. It was common for us to eat lunch in her classroom and talk about all sorts of teen issues; like dating, grades, peer pressure, college ambitions, and other stuff. We welcomed her advice. She remained a trusted friend to many of us, even after we graduated. To this day, we still exchange Christmas cards and stay in touch. I also joined a small group that performed choral skits for local elementary schools, civic organizations, and nursing homes. Interestingly, I'd acquired a comfort level to perform in public settings while in high school. This proved very beneficial for me later in my life.

Our guidance counselors were also very helpful and constantly concerned about everyone's academic progress. They seemed to provide a little extra help to students with college-bound potential.

I believe the counselors and administrators wanted success stories to balance the many other distracting and negative stories that revolved around drugs, gang violence, teen pregnancy, and many other issues within our inner city high school. There seemed to be a healthy competition among the local high schools; not only the athletic competition, but an academic competitiveness that also drove their attentiveness. The counselors were genuinely interested in our future. They kept an eye on us and continually encouraged us to do our best, not just in our school work, but also in our activities within our neighborhoods and throughout the community. We were encouraged to support PTA fund raising activities, YMCA pancake breakfasts, club car washes at local businesses, and church fish fries.

The counselors and administrators also earnestly helped those students who were not college-bound. They looked after students who didn't have money, had low grades, low SAT scores—or for any number of other reasons—needed jobs during or immediately after high school. Counselors helped those kids get into school-to-work programs, prepared them to enter the local technical schools, and other job training programs. Overall, the administrators, teachers, and counselors kept many students focused on their school work, while encouraging them to stay out of trouble. Many welcomed their help, encouragement, and support. Unfortunately, some did not. I remember one of my very bright classmates who became a gang leader's girlfriend. She was one of several pregnant girls who walked across the stage at graduation. I also remember a couple of other classmates who had to drop out of school. They had to get jobs to help their families pay rent, buy food and keep the lights on. For them, a part-time job turned into their full-time occupation because of their tough family situation.

Even the gang members recognized the importance of school. Essentially, the various student groups and opposing gangs had a sort of *you leave me alone and I'll leave you alone* status quo perspective during school hours. Frankly, I believe the gang members were just as book smart as they were street-smart, but they couldn't show it. With few exceptions, they knew to avoid bringing negative attention to themselves from school administrators or our on-campus cops (resource officers). Most of the time they avoided trouble and understood that school was an important social outlet for them too. It provided a routine they didn't have at home. For some, school was a place to escape their disruptive or abusive family life and offered an environment that had organization, routine, and rules. They could interact with one another in a place safer than the streets of their neighborhood. Unfortunately, not all gang members understood this critical concept. Their fist fights, knife fights, rude behavior or bathroom marijuana busts, quickly got them expelled. Most were sent to the county's alternative school called Gompers High School. I drove by it a few times just to see where it was and what it looked like. It reminded me of a prison. I didn't want to see the inside.

CHAPTER 6

Reach for The Moon

*"If you think you can, or you think you can't,
you're probably right!"*

~ Henry Ford

My hodge-podge group of high school classmates avoided any real trouble, except some typical teen mischief and pranks. We'd roll a friend's house and yard with toilet paper, smear shaving cream on a buddy's car on their birthday, or throw rotten eggs at one another in a local park on Halloween. At a few of our parties someone would sneak in some beer, Mad Dog 20-20 wine, or a couple of brown-bag bottles of whiskey. The liquid courage often ended the night with yelling and a few fist fights. At one party I drank some rum but threw up shortly after getting home. The next morning, my parents had one of those we're-really-disappointed-in-you *looks* on their faces. We had a stern conversation about my poor decision to drink alcohol. I was mad at myself for disappointing them and really hated the terrible hangover and headache.

As I look back on my high school years, I've come to realize some important milestones that I'd experienced. I faced many potential distractions during that time, which could have shifted my focus away from my school work, grades, and desire to go to college. But I didn't let any of those very real distractions derail me from my goals. In hindsight, I recognized that while in high school I not only learned from my class work, but also gained an important perspective on those people who significantly impacted my future.

Whether it's during our high school years, or other times in our lives, we will all face periods of challenge and temptation. With help from others we'll get through them. Perhaps we're striving to achieve personal or professional goals but only making limited progress. Financial specialists look to solve revenue problems. Sales people look to close deals, and business leaders look to grow their businesses and gain market share. But none of them can achieve their objectives alone. Reminded of my own successes while writing this book, I realized that I'd met people who earnestly believed that if something had to be done, they singularly made it happen. This is absolutely **NOT** true! Frankly, people who have that perspective are foolish.

Let me explain what I mean. Imagine someone driving a car with hands firmly gripping the car's steering wheel. They confidently believe they have total control of the vehicle. Yet, this illusion of control is quickly blurred when the road curves, traffic builds, or other external factors change. They may think they need only squeeze the steering wheel more firmly to maintain control of the car and negotiate the roadway better. But there are so many other moving parts and external factors that impact the situation. Some of them include the weather conditions, other vehicles and drivers, the road surface, tire pressure, traction, speed, engine power, brake performance, and traffic signals. All of them impact the future direction and destination of the vehicle and driver.

That's how it was with me. Throughout my time in high school, I was confident that I had a firm grasp of my situation. I had achieved a level of success because of my academic efforts. I was the one who ultimately took the quizzes and tests, turned in the projects and wrote the papers. In reality, I did not succeed solely on my own efforts. I was merely a contributor to my future not the controller of it. Several people influenced my circumstances and directly contributed to the outcome.

My parents were contributors. They were supportive and encouraged my brother and me to continue our education through high school and beyond. I'm sure that part of their encouragement stemmed from their desire for us to accomplish something that they hadn't. In fact, I found my dad's GED (General Equivalency Degree) and my mother's high school diploma among the documents in their files. During my junior year and senior year, they seemed to have an even greater interest in my grades. Through their encouragement, I was near the top 10% of my senior class. The potential of going to college was real.

As graduation approached and as I thought about what I wanted to do after high school, a future career in the military also crossed my mind. Recall that until my father retired, I grew up around the trappings of the military; the uniforms, the parades, the unique military terminology, the saluting, and much more. That all still intrigued me.

RICHMOND UNIFIED SCHOOL DISTRICT — REPORT CARD

School Name	School Term	Counselor	Gd.	Adv.	Student Name
HARRY ELLS HIGH	SPRING 1976	ERICKSON C	11	305	WILLIAMS EDDIE

EXPLANATION OF MARKS
A — Outstanding achievement
B — Good achievement
C — Satisfactory achievement
D — Minimum achievement
F — Failure due to unsatisfactory achievement
I — Incomplete due to justifiable absence

EXPLANATION OF COMMENTS
X — Excellent progress
G — Good attitude/conduct
I — Showing some improvement
2 — Achievement is not up to apparent ability
3 — Absences/tardiness affecting school work
4 — Books/materials are not brought to class
5 — Assignments are incomplete or unsatisfactory
6 — Oral participation needed
7 — Inattentive/ wastes time/ does not follow directions
8 — Conduct in class is not satisfactory
9 — Please contact teacher through counselor

Per./Sect.	COURSE	1	2	Sem	Comments	TEACHER	Credits
0	GERMAN 3	A	B	B		TAKEDA E	5.0
1	ENGLISH 3	A	A	A		CONE J	5.0
2	PE BOYS	A	A	A		GUIDA L	5.0
3	TYPING 2	A	B	B		GOWEN A	5.0
4	ALGEBRA 2	B	C	B		MURPHY K	5.0
5	CHEMISTRY	B	B	A	G	HAWKS G	5.0

Normal credits for a semester are 10. You may keep this card for your records.

182.0 CREDITS EARNED. REQUIRED FOR GRADE 10=45, FOR GRADE 11=105, FOR GRADE 12=165.

RICHMOND UNIFIED SCHOOL DISTRICT — REPORT CARD

School Name	School Term	Counselor	Gd.	Adv.	Student Name
HARRY ELLS HIGH	SPRING 1977	ERICKSON, C.	12	515	WILLIAMS EDDIE

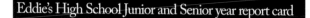

EXPLANATION OF MARKS
A — Outstanding achievement
B — Good achievement
C — Satisfactory achievement
D — Minimum achievement
F — Failure due to unsatisfactory achievement
I — Incomplete due to justifiable absence

EXPLANATION OF COMMENTS
X — Excellent progress
G — Good attitude/conduct
1 — Showing some improvement
2 — Achievement is not up to apparent ability
3 — Absences/tardiness affecting school work
4 — Books/materials are not brought to class
5 — Assignments are incomplete or unsatisfactory
6 — Oral participation needed
7 — Inattentive/ wastes time/ does not follow directions
8 — Conduct in class is not satisfactory
9 — Please contact teacher through counselor

Per./Sect.	COURSE	MARKS 1	2	Sem.	Comments	TEACHER	Credits
1	MATH ANALYS	A	B	A		MURPHY K	5•0
2	GERMAN 4	A	A	A		TAKEDA E	5•0
2	PHYSICS	C	C	C		MENGEL J	5•0
3	AMERCN GOVT	B	A	A		MCNICKLES JA	5•0
4	ENG ADV PLC	A	A	A		HEALY F	5•0
6	PE BOYS	A	A	A	X	ERKKILA W	5•0
7	STUDY HALL	A	A	A	XG	FINN M	5•0

Normal credits for a semester are 30. You may keep this card for your records.

Eddie's High School Junior and Senior year report card

By the time I was in high school, my dad had been out of the military for a couple of years. Because he was a military retiree our family had access to Oakland Army Base, Alameda Naval Base, and the Presidio in San Francisco. We regularly shopped at the Commissary (grocery store) or Post Exchange (department store) on those bases. On many of those trips, I saw soldiers and sailors with their duffle bags headed to or returning from Vietnam. Those visits made me think about a potential career in the military. In fact, one of the members of our church was a U.S. Navy Chief Petty Officer. One Saturday he'd gotten permission to give our church youth group a personal tour of his ship, the USS Enterprise (CVN-65). More than three football fields long, with hundreds of aircraft and thousands of sailors and Marines onboard, it was one of the biggest vessels in the U.S. Navy. The ship was impressive and our field trip made a military career even more appealing.

I have memories of the swanky dinners at the military base mess hall (cafeteria), especially during July 4th, Veterans Day, and Memorial Day holidays. We also went on fishing trips organized by the base Rod & Gun Club and summer family picnics put on by base commanders for soldiers and their families. It was during one of those picnics when I watched the Apollo 11 moon landing. Everyone crowded around someone's small black & white portable TV placed on top of a Volkswagen Van. I watched the grainy images of the moon landing, when astronaut Neil Armstrong took his famous first steps on the lunar surface. I also remember the images of when he and Buzz Aldrin planted the American flag. I felt the patriotism of the crowd as we cheered and celebrated such a wonderful achievement. During his 1961 address to the nation, President John F. Kennedy had set forth the auspicious national goal: the United States would *"land a man on the moon and return him safely to the earth by the end of the decade."* [10] It was achieved on a hot July day because of the wisdom, brilliance, and tremendous efforts of so many people working together. As a kid, I was one of the many proud Americans to witness that tremendous accomplishment!

As I tried to figure out what I wanted to do after graduation, my high school counselor, Mr. Clif Erickson, was also a great help. He took me under his wing. Like my parents, he must have seen college-bound potential in me. He often shared information with me about local colleges, such as the University of California campuses at San Francisco, Berkeley and Davis. He told me about other state schools, including CalTech, Stanford, UC San Diego, USC, and UCLA. With a good grade point average, a high senior class ranking, a respectable SAT score—which he made me take twice to get a better score—he and I narrowed my choices. I eventually applied to only two colleges. Both could not have been more diverse.

One was the University of California Berkley, renowned for being a respected but very liberal school. Many people may recall the anti-Vietnam War rallies, peace-nik activist movements, and other events on that campus throughout the 1960s and

70s. I had become quite familiar with the UC Berkley campus through a special program. This program allowed high school juniors and seniors with a high grade point average and who'd completed all of their core high school courses, to attend a few entry-level college classes on weekends and during the summer. The intent was to help transition college-bound students to a college environment. We also got a meal card and were paid a small stipend to help defray the cost of books, transportation, and as an incentive to do well in the program. I enjoyed the experience and got quite comfortable with the campus.

I also applied to the United States Military Academy at West Point, New York, a much more regimented and conservative school. As a very historic college, it was established to develop future military officers and leaders. Admission to West Point was quite competitive and required an appointment by a U.S. Senator or Congressman. Mr. Erickson helped me prepare appointment packets to my California Senators, Alan Cranston and John Tunney, and my local Congressman George Miller. He really helped me with the tedious admissions process for both colleges. He continuously kept me on track to get each school's applications completed and submitted by their deadline. We figured that I had a reasonable shot at getting accepted to both of them. Yet, they both had their respective positive and negative aspects.

UC Berkley was local and a one-hour bus ride away. I was familiar with the campus and college atmosphere because of the dual-enrollment program. I had the option to live at home or share an apartment near campus with a roommate. However, I learned from the admission material that UC Berkley's tuition was very expensive. West Point was in upstate New York, about fifty-miles north of New York City, and on the other side of the country. I had no family nearby. From the West Point admissions material it seemed quite challenging with very robust academic courses and a military oriented environment. Again, if I were accepted to West Point, how would I pay the tuition? Mr. Erickson helped me apply for scholarships and provided me with a lot of information on both schools. I had to read, understand, and balance each school's respective pros and cons.

I weighed the options of both schools. I had many critical questions to answer and would soon have to make very difficult decisions. Among them were did I want to attend college near my parents and stay in the Bay Area? Should I stay near my home where I had lots of friends and family for support or travel across the country to upstate New York, where I had no one? There were also other equally important personal factors that impacted my decision.

My brother had left home two years before. He decided to follow our dad's footsteps and enlisted in the U.S. Army. That left me as the only sibling at home. My parents were getting older and increasingly needed more medical care. If I stayed near home, I could still help drive them to their various doctor appointments at the Veteran's Administration (VA) hospital in San Francisco as well as to local grocery stores, military bases, and visit nearby relatives. My mother's rheumatoid arthritis and my dad's diabetes, bad back, and circulation problems in his legs were getting worse. I had to consider my parents' health conditions in my decision about college. Should I stay near them or seemingly abandon them by going to a college outside of California?

Clearly, another major consideration was college tuition. Though my parents never really talked about it, I knew we didn't have much family income. I'm certain they weren't able to save much money to help with my tuition and expenses. My father had retired as a U.S. Army Staff Sergeant so we had his military pension. He also worked another ten years for the U.S. Postal Service which added a little more to it. He was soon eligible for social security. My mother had been a stay-at-home mom, so my dad's pension and retirement was our family's only and fixed income.

That said, even though we had a limited income and weren't rich or even middle-class by any stretch of the imagination, we never lacked for anything. I knew my parents tried to put away some money for emergencies; car and home repairs, broken appliances, annual family vacations, or unexpected out of town trips. But I doubt they had enough savings set aside to cover the tremendous cost of college tuition. I think that my brother realized this well before I did, which is probably why he enlisted immediately after graduation. He had actually signed up for *delayed enlistment*. Since he had already turned eighteen, he could enlist before he graduated and then go to basic training afterward. I believe he wanted to get away from home, our parents, and me. He wanted to be on his own as soon as he could. Though my brother and I never talked about it, this was another one of those sibling issues I mentioned earlier.

As I soon faced important decisions about my future after high school, I also realized I'd learned to overcome many childhood challenges to this point. I could have let others' harsh and nasty comments negatively affect my self-esteem. I could have gotten caught up with the wrong crowd or joined a gang. I could have let those who questioned my *blackness* and mixed-race background impact my future ambitions. I could have believed those people who were rude and nasty to my family or let their ignorance prevent me from doing well in school. Yet, I didn't let any of those issues derail me as I prepared to graduate. It was critical for me to consider my future and weigh several important factors;

leaving my home and parents, which college to attend, and the future challenges of and after college.

Let me add one more consideration to my list. I'd discovered that West Point provided a U.S. Government backed full 4-year scholarship. However, the payback would be serving a minimum of five years as a U.S. Army officer after graduation. Also, because of West Point's traditions, highly respected curriculum, and rich history as a national institution, it was unbelievably competitive to get in. The academy received about twelve-thousand applications and accepted only about fourteen-hundred freshmen into the Corps of Cadets. Clearly, this meant that getting an appointment to West Point would be very difficult. Mr. Erickson got me information from the West Point admissions office. I read and re-read each brochure and course catalog a dozen times cover to cover. West Point's history, tradition, and lore impressed me. Though my chances of getting accepted were extremely small, I didn't let that stop me from trying.

Since it was founded in 1802, West Point has been recognized as one of the world's pre-eminent leader development schools. More than any other institution, the history of West Point was also the story of America. It holds a stellar reputation for developing leaders of character committed to the creed of *Duty, Honor, and Country*. Its graduates have greatly impacted all facets of American and world affairs. West Point alumni include; Ulysses S. Grant, Robert E. Lee, Stonewall Jackson, John J. Pershing, Douglas MacArthur, George C. Marshall, Dwight D. Eisenhower, Omar Bradley, George Patton, William Westmorland, Norman Schwarzkopf, David Petraeus, Martin Dempsey, and many other famous American military and civic leaders. America has repeatedly called upon West Point graduates for a wide spectrum of contributions, including; military operations, corporate management, and championing global projects. Additionally, West Point reinforced with each cadet that they are perpetually connected to all those who have graduated before them. Graduates are collectively part of one *long gray line* that stretches back to the very first class, and connects them all as a huge extended family in a common experience of service to the nation. This means that every graduate will always conduct themselves with unquestioned integrity, bringing honor to the academy in all of their dealings, and to those who have worn the cadet gray uniform and walked the same sacred ground of West Point. Cadets are required to adhere to the Cadet Honor Code; that *"a cadet will not lie, cheat, steal, nor tolerate those who do."* The academy bases a cadet's leadership experience as a development

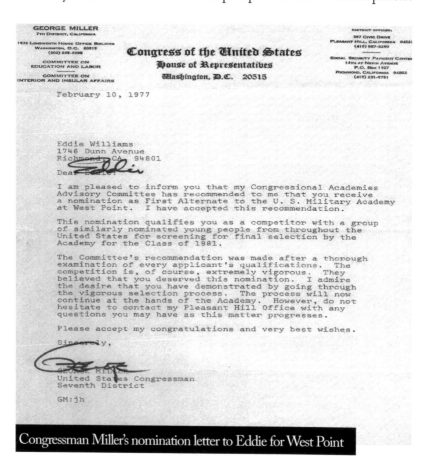

Congressman Miller's nomination letter to Eddie for West Point

of three pillars of performance: academics, physical, and military. If accepted to West Point would I be able to measure up to that high calling? Was I destined to join its elite group of alumni? If I were to attend West Point, would I survive the rigors of one of the most prestigious colleges in the world? Considering the large number of applicants and small percentage of admissions, the odds didn't look good.

In the spring of my high school senior year, I got letters of acceptance from both UC Berkeley and West Point. Now what was I going to do? Both colleges had their own appeal. Though I was thrilled, I had tough discussions with my parents, Mr. Erickson, and my teachers. After considering the full 4-year government scholarship, adventure, and history of the academy, West Point outweighed UC Berkley. I accepted the invitation to attend West Point.

Harry Ells proud of first West Pointer

By GORDON RADDUE
I-G Staff Writer

RICHMOND — Apprehensive? Not at all. But determined? Very much so.

That's the way Harry Ells High School senior Eddie Wiliams feels about his appointment to the United State Military Academy at West Point, N.Y.

Articulate and unaffected, 17-year-old Eddie has become the first student in Ells' 22-year history as a high school to receive an appointment to West Point.

In 1963 Pete Abbott and Tom Waller won respective appointments to the Air Force Academy in Colorado Springs, Colo., and the U. S. Naval Academy in Annapolis, Md., but Eddie is justifiably proud to be Ells' first West Pointer.

Equally proud are his father, retired Army S.Sgt. E-6 Foster Williams, and German-born mother, Lilli, who settled in Richmond seven years ago after years of service involved traveling together.

"We feel great about it," said the elder Williams, whose other son, Tommy, 21, is an Army sergeant stationed in Germany. "It's one of the greatest honors that can be bestowed on a son in America."

Although his mind had been set on an Army career for a long time, it wasn't until last spring that Eddie decided to try for West Point.

"I started thinking about college in my junior year," he said. "I wanted to get into the Army, so I thought, why not go for the top?"

He wrote Cong. George Miller's office that spring and, following a series of interviews and tests, was named first alternate on a list of West Point candidates.

"The Academy took it from there and gave me a direct appointment," said Eddie.

A lifetime member of the California Scholastic Federation (CSF) who carries a 3.6 grade point average, Eddie also was accepted for admittance to the University of California, Berkeley, but the challenge of West Point won out.

Why West Point?

"The leadership training, the academics, the traveling, the experience and the loyalty" were reasons he cited at random.

Loyalty is no small matter to Eddie. It extends to his family and to his school, especially to Ells' retiring principal, Elmer W. McCormick.

"I was particularly glad to do it (obtain the West Point appointment) in Mr. McCormick's last year," he said. "He's done a lot for the school."

"A classmate of mine, Michele Healy, has been accepted for Harvard," Eddie thoughtfully added. "Mr. McCormick will go out on a

(Turn to Page 4, Col. 2)

— I-G photo by Si Bailey

EDDIE WILLIAMS WITH ELLS PRINCIPAL ELMER McCORMICK
appointment a nice going-away present for retiring educator

Local newspaper article on me going to West Point
Source: Richmond Independent Newspaper

With that critical decision made, I was about to deal with many new challenges. I soon faced all of them on my own and on the other side of the country.

CHAPTER 7

Don't Quit

*"I wanted to say to young people, Look. Be where you are.
And if you don't like it, make some changes."*
~ **Maya Angelou**

My decision to leave the comfort of home, friends and parents to face the new challenges of West Point was difficult. Within a few days after graduation, I would join the new West Point freshman class and become a *Plebe*—the traditional term used for freshman cadets. My last few days at home were filled with anxiety and excitement about what the future held for me at the academy. Before leaving, a couple of my classmates hosted a going-away party for me. My parents were proud of what I'd accomplished by working hard in school and defying the odds to get admitted to West Point. They were also sad because the day when I would leave home had finally arrived. Though I was also proud of my accomplishment I was worried about them. I was leaving them behind with no one else at home to help with their health issues. It was now my turn to meet the adventures that lay ahead. The hour-long drive to the San Francisco Airport was quiet. None of us wanted to talk about the inevitable separation. As I kissed and hugged my parents before boarding the flight to New York, I felt a combination of exhilaration and fear. Many new questions crossed my mind. Would I regret my decision? Should I have stayed at home and near my parents? Should I have applied for more state and federal scholarships and attended UC Berkeley? Should I leave my family and friends behind and travel to the other side of the country? What would happen if my parents got injured and I wasn't around to help them? What do I do when their health gets worse? Would I be up to the tasks, challenges, and adventures of West Point and beyond?

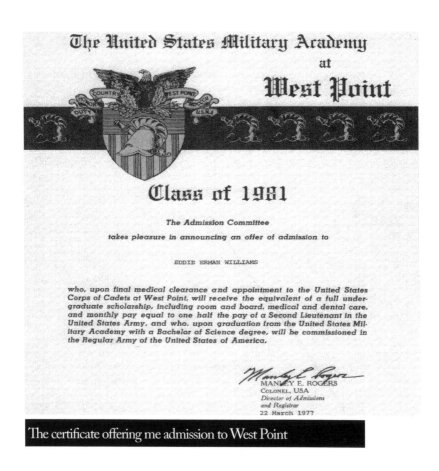

The certificate offering me admission to West Point

Even with all those questions, I had to face the fact that I'd made my decision to leave home and attend West Point. It was time to both look ahead and move forward. I was about to leave my comfort zone in a big way. I'm reminded of an ancient Chinese proverb;

Man cannot discover new oceans unless he has the courage to lose sight of the shore.

Have you had to make similar tough decisions? Have you failed to attempt something significant because you were uncertain about the outcome or how it would impact you or others you care about? You might have even regretted decisions or felt discouraged because of the unknown results? Maybe you felt that you didn't have the right amount of talent, connections, resources, or money to achieve the desired goal. Maybe it wasn't the right time to make those critical decisions. If this describes you, don't think that way any longer. Don't limit yourself!

I contend that the outcome of undertaking tough challenges, even if you don't always succeed at them, will actually teach you something critical about yourself. You will learn some important life-lessons because of the experience. At a minimum you will learn what you can actually achieve in the face of uncertainty or adversity. You can then use that knowledge when dealing with further challenges. Even if you fail, your attempt will bring some degree of success because of what you learned. There are several documented examples throughout history, of people overcoming challenges, disabilities, and failures that ultimately brought them success.

*Some of the world's greatest men and women have been saddled with disabilities and adversities, but managed to overcome them. Cripple him, and you have a **Sir Walter Scott.** Lock him in a prison cell, and you have **John Bunyan.** Bury him in the snows of Valley Forge, and you have **George Washington.** Raise him in abject poverty, and you have **Abraham Lincoln.** Subject him to bitter religious prejudice, and you have the diplomat **Benjamin Disraeli.** Strike him down with infantile paralysis, and he becomes a **Franklin D. Roosevelt.** Burn him so severely in a schoolhouse fire, that the doctors say he will never walk again, and you have **Glenn Cunningham;** who set a world's record in 1934 by running a mile in 4 minutes, 6.7 seconds. Deafen a genius composer, and you have **Ludwig van Beethoven.** Have him or her born black, in a society filled with racial discrimination, and you have **Booker T. Washington, Harriet Tubman, Marian Anderson, or George Washington Carver.** Make him the first child to survive in a poor Italian family of eighteen children, and you have **Enrico Caruso.** Have him born to parents who survived a Nazi concentration camp, paralyze him from the waist down when he is four, and you have the incomparable concert violinist, **Itzhak Perlman.** Call him a slow learner, retarded and write him off as un-educatable, and you have*

Albert Einstein. [11]

We all have to endure challenges and obstacles at some point in our lives. We have to make choices about how we must deal with them. You might be saying to yourself, *"But I'm not anything like those celebrities, diplomats, politicians, or athletes!"* You are absolutely right! You may be a CEO of a struggling business, or the provider for your family and just got laid off. You may be in a faltering relationship, or someone with overwhelming debt. You may have a life-threatening illness, or any number of other issues. Realize that ordinary people succeed in extraordinary ways, especially when faced with overwhelming challenges. Continue to believe in the success and survival of the human spirit to get through those challenges.

That said, there are some people who live below their potential. They have put their dreams on hold because of disappointments or setbacks. Successful people can't spend much time living in regret or condemnation from their failures. A friend once told me that there is a reason why a car's windshield is much bigger than the rearview mirror. He emphasized how people should focus on the road ahead. Never forget where you came from but don't dwell on it as you move forward. This is a thousand times harder to do, when you've rushed head long into the busyness of life and had failure along the way. It requires much more courage to not lose heart or lose hope and continue to seek new opportunities still ahead. Don't settle on the past but make the most of today and every tomorrow in front of you. We make choices all the time, every day. Always choose to keep moving forward. When you give of your time, your talent, and your resources, you're not just helping yourself. You reach out and help others, even people you don't know or may never meet. Take advantage of every opportunity that comes your way. Someone put it very well when they wrote:

Don't Quit

When things go wrong, as they sometimes will,
When the road you're trudging seems all uphill,

When the funds are low and the debts are high,
And you want to smile, but you have to sigh,
When care is pressing you down a bit–
Rest if you must, but don't you quit.

Life is weird with its twists and turns,
As every one of us sometimes learns,
And many a fellow turns about
When he might have won had he stuck it out.
Don't give up though the pace seems slow –
You may succeed with another blow.

Often the goal is nearer than
It seems to a faint and faltering man;
Often the struggler has given up
When he might have captured the victor's cup;
And he learned too late when the night came down,
How close he was to the golden crown.
Success is failure turned inside out
The silver tint in the clouds of doubt,
And you never can tell how close you are,
It might be near when it seems afar;
So stick to the fight when you're hardest hit –
It's when things seem worse that YOU MUST NOT QUIT.
~ Anonymous

Although we might not succeed at everything we attempt, that shouldn't frustrate us to the point that we stop trying. If this is you, redirect your energy, your efforts, and your time toward some other task or endeavor. Don't listen to those around you who are discouraging and negative. Even when the odds are against you, don't let that stop you from trying. Deflect or re-direct negativity. Re-focus any of your own doubts or *self-talk* toward achieving your goals. Make sure what we allow into our minds are not negative thoughts but uplifting ones. Invest in yourself. Learn something new. Realize that though you are not in control of everything, there are many things that you do control.

Here's an example of what I mean. You certainly wouldn't want to enter a marathon the first week you decide to start jogging. If you do, you're just setting yourself up for failure, disappointment, physical injury, or worse. Maybe the last time you wore a pair of running shoes was several years ago. But do not limit yourself in thinking that if you can't run a marathon right away, you shouldn't attempt it at all. Shift your focus to what you **CAN** do. Start exercising and jogging one day at a time. Begin by jogging for a block, then two, then three, until you've built up your endurance and stamina to eventually run the entire distance of 26.2 miles. What an achievement that would be.

It's just as critical to recognize that along the way toward achieving your goals, you'll have to deflect those who are not supportive. Those nay-sayers and negative thinkers you are certain to encounter. Those people who tell you that you can't do it. They laugh at you with contempt and enjoy your stumbles. They live to intimidate. They scoff at those who accept change. Those people are full of discouragement, depression, hopelessness, and dread. They are quick to tell you that you're fooling yourself if you think you can run a marathon. Prove them wrong! You don't need their "approval rating" or "dis-approval rating". Believe in yourself!

Let me make my point another way. Imagine that I somehow managed to break through all of the security measures at the U.S. Treasury at Fort Knox and obtained one of those valuable gold bricks. When I got home, I placed it on a shiny sterling silver platter, on top of a painstakingly hand-knitted doily. Then I sprinkled powdered sugar and scattered red rose pedals around the gold brick. Finally, I drove twenty miles through bumper-to-bumper traffic to get to a friend's house. After ringing the doorbell and with a smile on my face, I hand them this wonderful gift. Their response is, *"What is this … a gold brick? I can't do anything with that. Why did you want to give me a gold brick? No one can give me change for it at the grocery store. What in the world were you thinking? A gold brick … really! And by the way, I don't like red roses or powdered sugar either!"*

This example might be extreme or maybe it accurately describes someone you know. You may have a family member, business associate, co-worker, or even a friend who constantly focuses on the negative aspects of everything…and I mean everything. I call them *quackers*. They simply quack at anything and everything. Sometimes they quack just to hear themselves quack. Then they quack again and then quack some more. We may not know why they hang on to this constant bitterness, but they seem to nurse resentment and even cultivate it. They seem to have only negativity flowing through their veins. Regardless of what we do for them or say to them, they constantly respond with negative, caustic, depressing, and demeaning words or actions. Don't be like them! If at all possible, avoid them! Those people want nothing more than to build a following of fellow negative thinking quackers! Don't let that happen to you.

As I looked toward leaving the comforts of California, my family, friends, and familiar surroundings for the uncertainly of West Point, I got very encouraging comments from them. They wished me luck, told me that I'd do just fine, and wanted updates on my progress. From others, I heard *quacker* comments. Some of them were, *"It's too cold in New York and you're a California boy"*, *"But, you don't know anyone there. Will you be ok?"*, *"Wow – that sure is a long way from home."*, *"West Point, I heard that's a really tough school"* and, *"Are you sure that's what you really want to do?"*

The sarcasm dripped from their words. Sure, I was scared about this new and uncertain adventure, but I didn't let their comments deter my decision to boldly begin the next chapter of my life.

CHAPTER 8

The Greatest Generation

"Success is to be measured not so much by the position that one has reached in life as by the obstacles which he has overcome."
~ Booker T. Washington

Maybe you're familiar with the saying: *when one door closes another one opens.* The other door can be a different opportunity, another job, a new relationship or an entry-way to a new situation. The challenges you face while getting through the doorway might be stepping stones to a better future. Be encouraged. Each of us can reach our goals to rise higher and become stronger as a result of dealing with the challenges life gives us.

As I headed toward my new challenges at West Point, I thought I had a reasonable idea about what awaited me there. Remember, I was raised in a military family and had read a bunch of information about the academy. But being a military dependent— also known as a military brat—was very different than actually being in the military. I was familiar with the military traditions and regimented lifestyle. I also understood the challenges of frequently moving between military bases, having to make new friends, and constantly adapting to new surroundings. Though I didn't fully know all of the things that were ahead of me, my parents had given me a foundation of dealing with adversity, and had modeled self-confidence in dealing with a variety of issues.

I was born in a local hospital in Nürnberg, Germany. My family lived there for about five years until my father was reassigned to Fort Ord, California, near Monterey. You might think that since my father was American and my mother was German, that we spoke both English and German in our home. But we did not, for an extremely important reason. My mother was not an American citizen when she married my dad. To become a U.S. Citizen, she had to learn English and pass the U.S. citizenship test. She wanted to become an American citizen not just for her own benefit, but because this would then allow my brother and me to become naturalized American citizens. Toward that goal, my mother spoke very little German. She literally forced herself to speak and learn English as quickly as possible. My dad often quizzed her on the citizenship questions. Her efforts and discipline

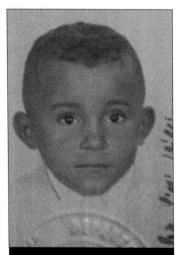

paid off. Within a few months, she learned English—though with a heavy German accent—and passed the citizenship test on her first attempt. After a few years at Fort Ord, my dad was re-assigned to Ft. Meade in Maryland. We lived there for about three years. My dad eventually retired from there after his honorable career of military service in the U.S. Army.

Eddie's U.S. Naturalization Certificate photo

My dad looking sharp on his Department of the Army (DA) photo

Recall that my dad had served in World War II. Like many Americans, his service demonstrated his generation's patriotism. The esteemed news anchor and journalist Tom Brokaw was absolutely correct in labeling the men and women who devoted themselves to selfless service to our country during that time, as *the greatest generation.* My dad was a member of that illustrious group. Brokaw so aptly wrote of them in his book, *The Greatest Generation.*

When the United States entered World War II, the U.S. government turned to ordinary Americans and asked of them extraordinary service, sacrifice, and heroics. Many Americans met those high expectations, and then returned home to lead ordinary lives.

When the war ended, more than twelve million men and women put their uniforms aside and returned to civilian life ... They weren't widely known outside their families or their communities ... They were proud of what they accomplished but they rarely discussed their experiences, even with each other. They became once again ordinary people, the kind of men and women who always have been the foundation of the American way of life. [12]

My dad also served during the Korean conflict. By the time we'd gotten to Fort Meade, MD, my dad had served a lengthy career in the U.S. Army. He had survived two wars and might again be called upon to serve in Vietnam. I recall my parent's conversations about America's escalating involvement in Vietnam while we watched the evening news coverage of the war. We had several family discussions about how the war might impact my dad and our family. A couple of my friends had their dad's sent to Vietnam. One had his dad killed there. Our family went to his home to console his family. Doing that made me concerned about my dad's potential deployment to his third war. I believe that it was a risk my parents didn't want to take. My dad had served long enough in the U.S. Army to retire and for our family to get retirement benefits. Also, as my brother and I approached our teen years, I think he wanted to be around us more.

After his military career ended, my dad started his new civilian career. We packed up our Chevy sedan and drove cross-country from Maryland to California. One of my dad's sisters lived in Richmond. After being in the military and away from his sister for several years, I guess he wanted to bring his family closer to her family. My aunt was a real estate agent. She knew people who could help him get a civilian job. My dad also had an older sister who lived in Oregon. My parents must have certainly considered that being near family would help stabilize our transition at this critical time.

Their decision also showed their strong resolve for a more stable future for our family. They knew we'd have to go through another cycle of new schools, new homes, and new friends. My parents also wanted us to be near relatives so they could help us adjust to the radical change of leaving the military lifestyle and adjust to the civilian world. I'm certain that my parents were concerned about how accommodating, or not, the civilian world would be to our bi-racial family. Being close to relatives would be both a buffer and helpful for us.

Here's what I mean. When President Truman integrated the military in the late-1940s, he required conformity. All service members—regardless of skin color—had to abide by the norms, policies, and decorum of the military. The civilian world lagged behind in adopting these concepts. The Civil Rights Movement of the 1960s was tumultuous in America because it tried to level the playing field for Americans of any color, as the military had done decades earlier. In short, people of different cultures were still likely to be subjected to others' harsh behavior, unequal treatment and unwillingness to compromise about getting along with those of a different color. At a time when our family was entering the civilian world, some people in American society were still unwilling or unable to accept equal rights, let alone accept mixed-race relationships and marriages. Our parents raised my brother and me to respect people, and not be offended by what some of them might say or do. I can only think that as we left the relative *safety net* of the military, they wanted us to have supportive family around, to help us all deal with the rude comments and inevitable abuse we were certain to encounter.

One of those times happened when my mother and I were shopping in a local grocery store. We'd gotten the customary stares, finger points, and harsh comments the entire time we were in the store. I pushed the grocery cart while my mother filled it. All of a sudden I saw that *look* come over her face. On that day, at that particular instant, she must have had enough of the gawkers and their not so subtle whispers. She calmly looked in their direction and said in her newly mastered English— albeit with a German accent, *"Take a picture ... it will last longer!"* Then, she turned around, grabbed the shopping cart gesturing me to follow her, and continued shopping. She didn't miss a beat in her routine.

I was too young to fully understand the significance of that particular moment or the deeper meaning of my mom's words. But I have never forgotten the event. I can now look back with absolute respect and clarity at her courage that day. My mother had modeled for me her best resistance against aggression. She gave no ground to the offensiveness of others. Her response displayed her character rather than the impulse to respond to evil with evil.

My parents continually taught me that it was a person's own strengths or ignorance that caused them to act in certain ways toward us. It wasn't because of anything I did or didn't do. As a child I was too young to fully grasp all of the dynamics that caused other people's actions or their words. Often when I heard their jeers, comments, and harsh words, I just wondered why they were so rude and nasty. In the way they handled so many uncomfortable events—like the grocery store incident—my parents modeled for me what to do when people were rude. In so many similar situations and events, I watched how they reacted to people's stupidity. I learned not to overreact or do something equally stupid myself. Through their calm and calculated reactions toward others' actions, my mom and dad often demonstrated for me the appropriate way to respond.

Me (riding tri-cycle), my older brother Tommy, and Mom while we were at Ft Ord, CA

I must have inherited my mother's endurance and strong character, and my dad's determination and strength, because I would certainly need it as I entered the front gates of West Point.

98

CHAPTER 9

"Yes sir", "No Sir", "No Excuse Sir", and "Sir I do not understand."

"If we take care of the minutes,
The years will take care of themselves."
~ Benjamin Franklin

I reported to West Point like so many before me, holding a small bag of basic toiletries and a check for other incidentals. Everything else I would need at the academy was issued to me. I expected to learn a system of values; honesty, integrity, selfless service, and leadership, that would not only impact me while there, but throughout my future military service and life. As soon as I entered the academy's front gates, I knew I was entering another world; a campus of gothic buildings, manicured lawns, spit-shined shoes, polished brass, crisp uniforms, military bands, and dozens of statues honoring so many of America's heroes. That first day—*called R-Day (Reception Day)*—was a blur of activity for me.

I recall the assembly for all of the incoming cadets and family members who were able to attend. We heard brief remarks from the Commandant as he welcomed us and acknowledged our hard work to get admitted. He briefed us on what we were about to go through during the next few weeks of new cadet training. He then asked the family members to hug or kiss their kids farewell. We were then herded off to be grilled by upperclassmen on how to march, salute, eat, and even talk. As new cadets, we only had four appropriate responses to upperclassmen: *"Yes sir", "No Sir", "No Excuse Sir", and "Sir I do not understand."* I'm sure all of us were scared during those first two months of initial training (called Beast Barracks). The training adjusted us to military life, basic soldier skills and requirements, allowed us to identify with West Point and its systems, and undergo administrative processing. As I collapsed on my bunk bed late each night—with only a few hours of sleep to prepare to do it all again the next day—I seriously wondered whether I'd measure up. Not only whether I could handle the harsh barks of upper-class cadets telling me not only what I could and couldn't do, but also whether I'd survive the academic, military, and physical demands of West Point over the next four years.

The academy's administration required that all cadets study subjects of a broad curriculum. It was called the *whole cadet concept.* Cadets were expected to be well versed in several different topics including; liberal arts, engineering, science, foreign language, public policy, and current affairs. We also participated in several different sports, in order to be well rounded *student-athletes* during our time at the academy. As future U.S. Army officers, cadets were expected to be competent and confident; whether at a dinner party with dignitaries and diplomats, in meetings with foreign heads of state, giving presentations to legislators and corporate executives, briefing top military brass, or leading soldiers in combat.

> **West Point's Mission:**
> *To educate, train and inspire the Corps of Cadets so that each graduate is a commissioned leader of character committed to the values of Duty, Honor, Country and prepared for a career of professional excellence and service to the Nation as an officer in the United States Army.* [13]

See Glossary of Common West Point Terms in Appendix 1.

I quickly realized that most of my classmates excelled both academically and physically in everything the academy threw at us. Many were varsity athletes (letter winners or Team Captains), Eagle Scouts, high school class valedictorians or salutatorians, national honor society members, national merit scholars, student body presidents, and heavily involved in a variety of community activities. They came from all over the country. Like me, some had family members with military backgrounds. A few had several generations of West Point graduates in their family history. Those who did not were beginning their own legacy of military service. Frankly, most of my classmates were much smarter, more gifted, and far more athletic than me. The fourteen-hundred new cadets were certainly the cream of the crop.

I now understood why the West Point admissions process was purposely difficult. Incoming cadets needed strong foundational academic and athletic skills to handle the rigors of the academy. It didn't take long for me to discover the big differences between me and many of my classmates. Being in the top percentile of my inner-city high school in Richmond, California was quite different from being in the top percentile of my exceptionally smart and athletic academy classmates—who came from up-scale communities and big city high schools all over the country. A few came from various countries around the world. I'm sure those nations would only send their best and brightest to represent them at West Point.

The mental and physical demands placed on every cadet required the ability to effectively multi-task and quickly grasp new concepts and skills. In all honesty, I lacked the effective study habits I needed to academically compete in my coursework. The study skills I brought were far short of what I would need to survive West Point. Frankly, if I didn't quickly learn how to learn, I would soon be on my way back home to California. I studied very hard, all the time and everyday—including weekends. I established a study routine where after reading the class assignments and hearing the instructors' lectures, I would then re-read and review the material several more times in my dorm room (called barracks). Only then would the material finally register and make sense. I often got extra help either from instructors who conducted study halls (called additional instruction or "AI") or from my much smarter classmates.

Mom and me during Christmas break of my freshman (plebe) year

With all of the academic and physical demands of West Point, cadets only survived its rigors by working together. Teamwork was an absolutely integral part of cadet daily life. West Point was a literal incubator of Darwin's saying:

It is not the strongest of the species that survives, not the most intelligent, but rather the one most responsive to change. [14]

Though cadets competed for class ranking, we simultaneously helped each other with the variety of academics, leadership positions, athletics, cadet duties, and numerous other activities. No one could get through *the West Point experience* solely on their individual efforts. In fact, life-long bonds were quickly formed because of the camaraderie among cadets and from enduring the challenges of cadet life. West Point discouraged success solely based on individual achievement and had little leniency for academic failure.

Each of West Point's academic courses were tough. Throughout my plebe year all of my grades consistently hovered just above passing. If it wasn't for my AI sessions and partial credit; where instructors gave me credit for the steps to get to the correct answer even if it was way off the mark, I would have failed. English and Calculus were my most difficult subjects. Going into the final exams, I was certain I wasn't going to pass either of them. My final grade in both proved that my persistence and long hours of review had paid off. Some of the saddest moments at the end of my plebe year were saying goodbye to a couple of my friends and classmates who'd failed one or more classes. Along with coursework, each plebe's life was filled with numerous activities requiring much of our time, energy, and effort. Plebes performed duties for upper-class cadets, such as: delivering mail, picking up and delivering dry cleaned uniforms and laundry, announcing the daily cadet formations (assemblies for accountability before meals or special events) and other duties. A traditional right of passage for plebes required the memorization of a wide range of information, and accurately reciting the details when requested by any upperclassman. The objective of this exercise, according to the guidebook (called Bugle Notes) was to develop memory retention skills and the ability to perform under pressure. Many years later, I can still recall the intense pressure of a demand from any upperclassman, and then having to immediately recite from memory any number of cadet knowledge (called Poop). Some of it was specific to West Point traditions, songs, or speeches. Other required poop was a summary of the front page of the New York Times newspaper, and countless other pieces of military lore. Here are a couple of examples,

Question: *What did General Sherman, Class of 1840, say of war?*

Answer: *There is many a boy who looks on war as all glory, but boys, it is all hell.*

Question: *Who discovered the source of the Mississippi River?*

Answer: *2nd Lieutenant James Allen, Class of 1829, discovered the sources of the Mississippi River in 1833.*

(Source: West Point Bugle Notes, 1977)

Cadets wore several different uniforms for the various events and activities, including different uniforms for class, and seasonal uniforms for ceremonies and parades. There were also specific uniforms for formal and informal meals in the huge dining hall (called the Mess Hall) which accommodated over four-thousand cadets for three meals each day. Plebes also served upperclassmen through a variety of duties at the meal table. They included announcing the dessert, accurately cutting any pie or cake for the exact number of cadets desiring it, as well as, announcing and serving the hot and cold beverages. Plebes could eat only after all the upperclassmen on the table had been served and then only after permission was granted by the senior ranking cadet. Plebes also ate in a specific fashion, called *square meals*. Food could not extend beyond the width and length of the fork. The fork was raised vertically from the plate and then horizontally to the mouth. Only after the fork was placed back on the plate could plebes chew their food. Plebes sat erect in their chairs with the space of a width of a fist between their chair back and their back. If any of the plebe table duties were not done satisfactorily, all the plebes on the table were subject to additional poop recitation, limited on the amount of time to eat, or both.

All cadet rooms were meticulous and always ready for inspection. The various uniforms were kept clean, pressed, and hung in a specific order. In fact, every piece of cadet clothing was folded, rolled and placed specifically in the dresser draw, closet, and foot locker. Every pair of shoes, every book, and even every toiletry item had their proper place in cadet rooms. Cadets had to constantly maintain spit-shined shoes, highly polished brass belt buckles, cap insignia, and uniform buttons. Beds were made so tightly that a quarter could bounce off the blanket. Depending on the severity of cadet offenses the typical punishment was either demerits or punishment tours. If a cadet got too many demerits, they could get expelled from West Point. To work off demerits, cadets were confined to their room—during what was normally their free time—except to go to the bathroom, meals, academic buildings, or the library. Punishment tours could also result in *Walking the Area*. This ruined a cadet's Saturday and Sunday afternoon because they had to walk back and forth in the open areas between barracks—while wearing full dress uniform with their rifle on their shoulder—for a specific number of hours matching their demerits. Some cadets were in the century club (one hundred or more hours) or double-century club.

Clearly, with all of the demands; time management, attention to detail, quickly grasp new concepts, rote responses to upperclassmen,  and supporting classmates— every plebe's day was intentionally overwhelming. Teamwork was essential to survive all of these requirements. Everyone had to work together, all the time, and every day. Those plebes who could not handle it were quickly weeded out.

Cadet Williams in his room just before participating in a "full dress" uniform parade

Roughly thirty percent of each cadet class dropout during their four-year period at West Point. In fact, during the Commandant's briefing on that first day, I recall his sobering comment to the new cadets and their family members. He said, *"Look to your right, now look to your left. Within the next four years, one of you won't be here"*. Traditionally most cadets leave during their plebe year because it's the toughest; given all of the adjustments to cadet life, plebe duties, academic load, demerits, violation of the *cadet honor code*, and home sickness. The primary reason was academic failure (called *going-D* or going deficient) in at least one subject. The academic rigors combined with all of the duties, functions, and time constraints on all cadets—freshmen through senior year—took its toll.

Occasionally, a few select cadets were *turned-back* or allowed to join the class behind them. During summer school they had to retake the class they'd failed, as long as there were acceptable mitigating circumstances which caused the failure; such as extended illness, injury or a lengthy family emergency. Those cadets would be able to stay at West Point so long as their demonstrated leadership, decorum, and disciplinary standing supported it. Though I constantly struggled academically at West Point, I survived because of the support from my classmates—especially several very smart roommates. Again, the course material was tough. My roommates helped by re-explaining the course material in different ways, proofreading my papers, quizzing me before tests, and helping me work out sample problems.

In fact, I was convinced that my junior year roommate was an absolute genius. He was one of those people who had the uncanny ability to grasp course material as soon as the words left the instructor's mouth. He rarely cracked a book or took notes. He spent most of his time in our barracks room listening to music, working on advanced projects, or helping me. I'm sure I drove him crazy, constantly asking him to help me study. He was so smart that he literally built a computer as his Advanced Electrical Engineering project. He drew the schematics and worked on component parts in our barracks room. Then he tested and assembled them in the Electrical Engineering lab. I barely understood what a computer was, what it did, or how it worked. He built one.

Every cadet was also required to participate in a variety of sports. West Point had several varsity sports and numerous cadets were specifically recruited for the football, basketball, cross county, gymnastics, hockey, and a variety of other teams. All other cadets participated in intramural sports such as, lacrosse, soccer, and track. The Corps was divided into thirty-six companies. Those companies were divided into four (nine company) regiments. Company intramural teams competed within their regiment. All cadets were also required to take Physical Education (PE) classes in sports, such as racquetball, swimming, boxing and golf. All plebes had to take boxing. I've never forgotten those first punches I took in my face, and how quickly I learned to defend myself and build self-confidence. I liked to box and participated in my company's intramural team. My boxing record was eleven wins and one loss.

Each year every cadet had to participate in a rigorous Indoor Obstacle Course Test (IOCT) which was a timed, physically-challenging event. The IOCT tested full-body physical fitness. It was both feared and revered. Candidly, it was so hard it

The Company A, 3rd Regiment Intramural Track team my senior year

nearly killed me every time I did it. The test consisted of eleven events performed sequentially: low crawl under barrier, tire footwork, two-handed vault, 8 ft. horizontal shelf, horizontal bar navigation, hanging tire, balance beam, 8 ft. horizontal wall, 20 ft. horizontal ladder, 16 ft. vertical rope, and 350m sprint (carrying a 6 lb. medicine ball for the first 120m, a baton for the second 120m, and empty-handed for the remaining 110m). It holds a special place in the hearts of every cadet. It was common for cadets to have the IOCT *cough and wheeze* for several days afterward. Along with maintaining the U. S. Army height and weight standard, we were also required to annually take and excel at the U.S. Army Physical Fitness Test (APFT). It consisted of three events: two minutes of Pushups, two minutes of Sit-ups, and a two-mile run. The two-mile run was conducted along a road on the lower portion of the academy campus next to the Hudson River and by the sewage treatment plant. That event also holds a fond memory for every cadet.

All of this established the many academic and physical challenges I faced at West Point. I had to compete and survive among very smart, very athletic, and far more capable classmates. I'm sure at some point every cadet asked themselves whether they had the ability to academically and physically endure the rigors of the academy. I endured by staying focused on getting through the challenges of each day, passing each course, maintaining my health and physical fitness, supporting and being supported by classmates, while appreciating the experience of being there.

I realized early on and continuously as a cadet, that whatever I lacked in academic skill and athletic prowess, I'd have to overcome with sheer determination. Many cadets before me had survived West Point. Since 1802, West Point has had a long line of graduates. I'm sure many of them overcame their own academic and athletic challenges. I wanted to add my name to that list of alumni and fulfill a personal goal. I also didn't want to disappoint my parents, teachers, high school counselors, and family who had helped me get into West Point.

Cadets earn leadership positions within the Corps and are given increased levels of responsibility, based on a combination of their academic standing, observed and demonstrated leadership potential, and the evaluations from their company Tactical Officer (TAC). The TACs, often academy graduates themselves, were seasoned commissioned officers assigned to West Point, and charged to assist, counsel, mentor, model leadership behavior, decorum and prepare cadets to lead soldiers upon commissioning. The competitiveness of West Point revolved around constant evaluation, physical and academic rigor, and continuous learning. Successes—even mistakes—were welcomed so long as growth and development was achieved. My determination to do well quickly proved beneficial.

During the summer between my sophomore (called Yearling) and junior (called Cow) year and based on my demonstrated leadership potential and evaluations, I was one of thirty cadets selected to attend the U.S. Army Ranger School. We went through the course with U.S. Army soldiers. The sixty-day Ranger School course was an intense combat leadership program oriented toward small-unit tactics. It required top physical condition because of the fast-paced training. We received instruction on military mountaineering tasks and techniques to employ squads and platoons for continuous combat patrol operations in a mountainous environment. Further training developed command and control in platoon-sized patrols through planning, preparing and executing a variety of day and night combat patrol missions. We had to be capable of operating effectively under conditions of extreme mental and physical stress. During the course most of us lost at least twenty pounds.

We conducted a variety of exercises in extended patrol operations in small units on airborne, air assault, small boat, ship-to-shore, and dismounted combat patrol operations against a well-trained and sophisticated simulated enemy. Several Ranger students, cadets and soldiers alike, were injured, quit, failed critical tests or didn't pass enough patrols. They were sent back to their units. It was such a personal thrill when most of my academy classmates and I completed the course. We were awarded and able to wear the coveted black and gold Ranger Tab on our cadet uniforms. We had completed one of the U.S. Army's most grueling courses.

During the summer between my junior year and senior year, I was selected to be one of twenty Cadet Company Commanders to train sophomore cadets in their summer training. Senior cadets (called Firsties) organized, managed and coordinated

Ranger Class 503-79, Ranger Williams is 5th row from front, 6th from right

eight weeks of field training at Camp Buckner, on the West Point military Reservation, and at Fort Knox, Kentucky. This rigorous training familiarized sophomore cadets with basic and advanced individual soldier skills. They were introduced to the combat, combat support and combat service support branches of the U.S. Army. As the Company Commander for 6th Cadet Field Training Company, I was responsible to direct my cadet staff as we trained several hundred Yearlings. Clearly, this responsibility helped me further develop my leadership and management skills.

Within the entire four-thousand members of the Corps of Cadets, sixteen senior cadets assume the additional responsibilities of various top leadership positions. These cadets modeled and monitored cadet behavior and discipline, took charge of formations, parades, and other critical areas of cadet life. They had opportunities to practice leadership within the upper echelon of the cadet chain of command, utilize effective communication and sound organization skills based on their demonstrated abilities during their previous three years. During my senior year, I was selected as one of those sixteen cadets because of the observations and evaluation of my peers, TACs, and Instructors on my leadership potential, physical aptitude, and academic performance.

As a member of the Brigade staff, my cadet rank was Brigade Command Sergeant Major. Essentially, I was the highest ranking enlisted cadet

Eddie (back row, second from left) on Brigade Staff. Source: Howitzer Yearbook 1981

within the entire Corps. My cadet boss was the highest ranking officer cadet; the Cadet First Captain. Each of the Brigade Staff members still had all of our normal academic and athletic responsibilities, with additional leadership duties that directly impacted the day-to-day functions of the entire Corps. I was responsible for a number of specific functions. They included ensuring the Colors; (National Flag, U.S. Army Flag, West Point Flag, and General Officer Flags), were protected, properly maintained and correctly displayed during the numerous academy parades, events, ceremonies, and functions. I also planned and coordinated cadet guides for numerous tour groups, VIP's, and guests who visited West Point. Diplomats, top military brass, celebrities, and politicians frequently held meetings and conferences at the academy. West Point was a popular venue for national and international discussions and forums. The academy was also a popular tourist attraction because of its history, picturesque location on the banks of the Hudson River, and scenic campus. Parades of crisply uniformed cadets marching to the tunes of military bands occurred nearly every Saturday and weekday afternoon. Candidly, because we had so many other things to do, cadets were often heard yelling a traditional chant called *"O-den,"* in hopes of creating rain showers to cancel parades. Sometimes the chants worked and sometimes they didn't. But it was interesting to hear several thousand cadets, each calling out "O-den" from their barracks windows to bring rain and free up some time.

One of my most vivid memories as Brigade Command Sergeant Major was being part of a select group of cadets, tasked to help coordinate the homecoming activities and chapel services for the American hostages held in Iran for four-hundred and forty-four days in 1979.[15] When finally released by Iran's Ayatollah Khomeini, the fifty-two hostages were flown from Iran to Germany for medical examinations. They then traveled to New York, where they were driven via a long bus convoy—the entire

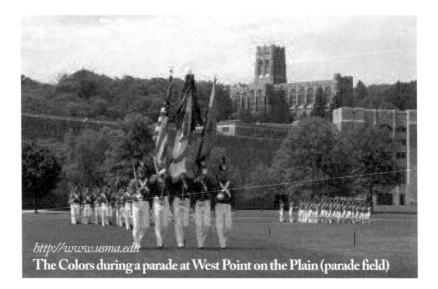

http://www.usma.edu
The Colors during a parade at West Point on the Plain (parade field)

route lined with yellow ribbons—to West Point, for private reunions with their families. This was a thrilling event for me because I had kept up with news accounts of the diplomatic efforts to release them. It was an honor to assist such a national outpouring of American patriotism for the returning hostages. Candidly, participating in the event increased my determination to complete West Point and serve America as a future officer in the United States Army.

As graduation approached, I was awash in all of the traditions of the Academy's illustrious history. I was about to complete my four years of academic, leadership and athletic rigor. I'd completed the traditions so many others had done before me; plebe duties, various summer training, Army-Navy football games, leadership positions, the IOCT, countless parades, hundreds of inspections, punishment tours, and many other events. I experienced a flood of emotions as I looked back on my time there. Those emotions ranged from boredom during the gray gloomy days of upstate New York winters, to sheer elation on surviving four long years of West Point's demands.

I especially recall attending an alumni reception during graduation week. Graduates and former cadets were invited back for reunions and various festivities. During an alumni dinner at the Thayer Hotel dining room, I had a brief but truly memorable conversation with a graduate from the West Point class of 1915. The gentleman was about ninety years old. A couple of his classmates were President Dwight Eisenhower and General Omar Bradley. In fact, his class was respectfully known the *class that stars fell on* because so many generals came from his cadet class.

Though he walked slowly and spoke softly his mind was very sharp. We chatted for only a few minutes about the meaningful experience we'd both had during our respective time as cadets. Though we'd attended West Point more than sixty-five years apart, we were able to relate to having very similar experiences. We had so much in common: Similar feelings of fear and nervousness on that first day at West Point, frustration with performing Plebe duties for upperclassmen, difficulties with our academic classes, physical strain from all of the athletic demands, homesickness, and so many other common perspectives. It was as if he and I were classmates. He shook my hand and congratulated me on making it through West Point. That hand shake was extremely meaningful for me. It validated that I had accomplished the right-of-passage to become a member of the *long gray line.*

Graduation day was a perfect spring day in late May. Thousands of people filled Michie Stadium to attend the ceremony. My parents traveled from California. My brother—now a Sergeant in the U.S. Army—and his wife made the trip from Germany. My aunt and uncle, who had helped our family transition after my dad retired, also came to watch me graduate. This was a special day for all of them too. Our guest speaker was President Ronald Reagan, who had just recovered from the assassination attempt only a few months before. With military precision, our class filed into our seats on the field and listened to a steady stream of congratulatory remarks from the Dean, Brigadier General Frederick Smith, the Commandant of Cadets, Brigadier General Joe Franklin, the Superintendent, Lieutenant General Andrew Goodpaster, and President Ronald Reagan. It was a pleasure to watch so many of my classmates and friends graduate. Except for the top ranked cadet, all other names were called alphabetically. I was thrilled when my name was finally called. After four long years, it was my turn to walk onto the stage to receive my diploma from the Commandant. I was awarded a Bachelor of Science degree in General Engineering and commissioned into the Infantry Branch as a Second Lieutenant (2LT) in the U.S. Army. For me, the occasion was even more poignant. While growing up, I'd been called epithets, shunned, spat at, and told I was a lie. On the way back to my seat, I was able to shake President Reagan's hand. He gripped my hand firmly, looked me in the eye and said, *"Congratulations Lieutenant"*. He was so gracious to allow each graduate a few moments with him.

Getting my diploma and tossing my cap into the air with my classmates that day was a tremendous accomplishment. When

Receiving my diploma from BG Franklin, the Commandant of Cadets

I finally found my family in the crowd there were hugs and kisses all around. Tears filled my parents' eyes as they congratulated me. My brother gave me my first salute. By tradition, I gave him a silver dollar coin in recognition of that honor. My aunt and uncle were thrilled and couldn't get enough of all the pomp and military ceremony of the event. I was especially overjoyed for my dad. Just a generation before that day, he had to have a U.S. Army officer approve his marriage to my mom and then they had to practically get married in secret. Now their youngest son was a graduate of America's highest institution that produced U.S. Army officers, and was openly welcomed by the President of the United States. What a day!

My academic standing was near the bottom of my class. Even though I was in the one-third that made the top two-thirds possible, my diploma contained the exact same citation that the very top graduate received:

Be it known that Eddie E. Williams has successfully completed the requirements for graduation from the United States Military Academy. In testimony whereof and by virtue of the authority vested in the Academic Board, we do confer upon him the degree of Bachelor of Science and recommend him to the President for appointment as a commissioned officer in the United States Army.

Clearly, surviving and graduating from West Point was the culmination of numerous physical and mental challenges. Four years earlier, I wondered about my ability to meet those challenges as I flew from California to West Point. Graduation day again reminded me of the Commandant's briefing on that very first day. He was right. My class entered with fourteen-hundred and sixty-five new cadets and graduated nine-hundred and sixty-three new officers. About a third of my class didn't make it. For me, graduation day demonstrated that I had also overcome that dubious statistic.

I had learned much and matured a great deal between the day I entered the academy's front gates alone, and when I saw those same gates diminish in the rear view mirror of the car with my family. I'd achieved much. Yet, an entirely new set of challenges and adventures were about to begin. After the glow of graduation too-quickly faded, new questions soon crept into my mind. Had I learned enough at West Point to effectively lead soldiers? How would I handle the next chapter in my life as a commissioned officer? What was ahead of me in the U.S. Army? Though I had raised my right hand, accepted my oath, signed on the dotted line, and agreed to fulfill my five-year obligation, was I prepared for all that was ahead of me?

CHAPTER 10

A Very Bad Landing

"I don't know the key to success,
but the key to failure is trying to please everybody."
~ Bill Cosby, Comedian

Graduating from West Point ended one significant phase in my life and opened the path to another. I was about to undertake new challenges as a freshly minted Second Lieutenant. I now had to apply my acquired academic, athletic, and leadership skill sets toward leading soldiers. Before beginning my military career, I spent time back home in California relaxing and re-connecting with my family and friends. I also enjoyed a week-long trip to Hawaii, taking a military *space available* (Space-A) flight from Travis Air Force Base, CA to Hickam Field, HI. That trip was my graduation present to me. I took advantage of all the things Hawaii was famous for: the beautiful beaches, majestic sunsets, warm weather, and friendly people. I also visited the USS Arizona memorial at Pearl Harbor, both to acknowledge the sacrifice that occurred on December 7, 1941, and also to reinforce to myself that freedom was not free. The final portion of my vacation (called *leave* in the military) was a cross-country drive from California to Georgia. I used the time to enjoy the sights and scenery of America and also to mentally prepare myself for the new adventures.

I had orders to attend the U.S. Army Airborne School, at Fort Benning, GA. The three weeks of *jump school* were both thrilling and scary. I had to trust that the military instructors were properly preparing me to safely do what was not natural; jump from a perfectly good aircraft and land safely. I also had to trust that the soldiers responsible to pack the parachutes (called riggers) had paid attention during their training and done their job properly. Finally, I had to trust myself. After voluntarily jumping out of the plane, and after the parachute opened, I would use proper technique to land safely. Getting my airborne wings was another milestone event in my life. It certainly helped me overcome my fear of heights which I had in common with my dad. While still at Fort Benning, I then attended the Infantry Officer Basic Course (IOBC). IOBC was a five-month course which taught newly commissioned infantry officers critical details about the Infantry Branch and provided in-depth training on how to be an effective junior infantry officer. Each U.S. Army branch; Armor, Infantry, Air Defense, Chemical Corps, Engineers, and others, have their own respective course for branch familiarization and training. The IOBC class was filled with other West Point classmates, along with ROTC graduates from all over the country,

and National Guard junior officers. IOBC allowed me to meet, interact, and train with numerous colleagues during the early stage of our profession.

In the field during IOBC (Ft. Benning, GA)

I was now prepared for what awaited me at my first assignment at Fort Stewart, Georgia, about an hour from Savannah. I was about to apply everything I'd learned at West Point and IOBC to the realities of the U.S. Army. I was confident in my own abilities, but also knew I would not be able to achieve success alone. I was prepared to apply what I'd learned, but willing to learn from my superior and fellow officers, sergeants (also called non-commissioned officers or NCOs) and soldiers. They would teach me many new lessons in leadership, how to accomplish assigned missions, how to multi-task, and how to effectively lead. At West Point, I'd spent four years acquiring foundational leadership skills. I'd also studied the personal attributes of numerous military leaders, analyzed lessons learned in many of history's battles and wars, and formed the basis for my own leadership style. I'd done so in the *controlled* environment of the academy. I was soon in a position to apply what I'd learned to the *real world* of the U.S. Army. I knew it was critical at this early stage to continuously build on my academy foundation. I would soon be responsible to train, prepare, and if ordered, lead soldiers in combat. Training for combat in the infantry required in-depth, accurate, appropriate, and quick decision-making. As an officer I needed to have tremendous physical and mental toughness as a leader, especially in times of confusion and chaos. I'd learned and acquired the skills and talents to be a competent officer. Would I be able to learn from veteran officers, NCOs, and soldiers and apply that knowledge toward being a leader? I was about to find out.

My first job was being an Infantry Platoon Leader, in charge of twenty-three soldiers of the 2nd Battalion, 34th Infantry Regiment of the 24th Mechanized Infantry Division (24th ID). I was directly responsible for their health, welfare, and training. One of the 24th ID's primary missions was to prepare thousands of soldiers for deployment to the Middle East. The U.S. Department of

Defense leadership's focus was there, because of the region's crude oil supply, the historic religious strife, and territorial conflicts between Israel and the surrounding Arab neighbors.

I enjoyed being a platoon leader. I was doing what I had been trained to do: prepare my soldiers to conduct our missions and carry out the orders of my superior officers and national leaders. Traditionally, officers provide guidance and issue orders and the NCOs execute the orders and make sure training got done and soldiers were prepared. As a new officer, I was mentored by an experienced Vietnam veteran and extremely knowledgeable Platoon Sergeant, Sergeant First Class (SFC) Warren Pippin. He managed the day-to-day activities and accountability of our platoon's troops, while I provided him guidance based on the directions and orders from my boss, the Company Commander.

We trained hard and continuously conducted a variety of daytime and nighttime exercises on the sprawling Fort Stewart reservation. We spent countless hours on the rifle ranges, machine gun ranges, and training areas honing our weapons skills and becoming proficient on small unit infantry tactics. We constantly trained to fulfill the basic infantry tenant; *shoot, move, and communicate.* We also traveled across the country to the newly established desert training area at the National Training Center (NTC), at Fort Irwin, California. NTC was created in the Mojave Desert for maneuver and weapons training in a desert environment. During our exercises we faced a highly skilled simulated enemy called Opposition Forces *(OPFOR)*. All vehicles were wired with electronic tracking devices so our actions were monitored and recorded on computers. All soldiers wore MILES laser equipment which allowed us to immediately know when we'd been shot or when our vehicles (Armored Personnel Carriers or APCs) were hit. During the after action reviews (AARs), all of the commanders, soldiers and exercise observers reviewed, evaluated, and analyzed each battle using the recorded data. The decisions, mistakes, and outcomes of each engagement were discussed in detail. These reviews were eye-opening and critical, but always in an atmosphere of learning what went right, what went wrong, and how could the engagement have gone better.

Conducting an AAR of the day's exercises with my Platoon NCO's at NTC, Ft. Irwin, CA

NTC's desert training area was different from the often swampy training area of Fort Stewart. It was sobering to train against a purposefully crafty and imposing OPFOR enemy, and in an environment similar to where our next major war would most likely occur.

I learned several important lessons at NTC—especially during one particular exercise. During that mission, my platoon's soldiers and our Armored Personnel Carriers (APCs) were positioned just below the crest of a long mountain range. We protected the flank of our task force. At the break of dawn, my radio operator and I looked over the crest just as the exercise started. Through my binoculars—which I held with my hands slightly over the front to prevent the sun from reflecting off the lenses and revealing our position—I saw the entire horizon filled with enemy OPFOR soldiers, tanks, and all sorts of vehicles. They were all heading at full speed in our direction. Before I could radio this information to my chain-of-command we were quickly

My Platoon's APCs looking for OPFOR at NTC

overwhelmed, outnumbered, and overrun. That particular after action review was quite sobering for all of us.

My platoon also conducted joint training with the 101st Air Assault Division at Fort Campbell, Kentucky. The U.S. Army leadership encouraged what they called *combined arms training*, where units of differing structure and equipment trained together, because they may potentially fight together in combat. Knowing various unit capabilities, limitations, strengths and weaknesses, made this type of training essential prior to deployment. Through all of this training, I became increasingly confident that my platoon was prepared for the contingency of war, and that I was competent to lead them as their Platoon Leader.

My Officer Evaluation Reports (OERs) from my bosses were very good. According to my commanders, I exhibited the requisite level of skill and knowledge necessary to be a capable junior officer. I was pleased with my evaluations at this early stage of my military career. Yet, I also became frustrated during my time at Fort Stewart. I wondered what the Army was doing positioning a Mechanized Infantry Division composed of hundreds of heavy tanks, artillery guns, APC's, and other vehicles in a place that was swampy and muddy most of the time. In fact, Fort Stewart was well known for the nickname, "Camp Swampy". It was difficult to maneuver our vehicles. I'd heard in numerous safety briefings how tanks and APCs often got stuck, flipped, or sank in the swamps and ponds when drivers ventured off the training area trails and roads. Also, APC's required an extraordinary amount of maintenance, especially when the tread (called tracks) around their wheels broke. The APC's engines were often over-stressed and blew because of the strain of maneuvering in the swampy areas. To that end, we conducted training specifically to practice amphibious operations. Swimming our multi-ton APCs was possible, but required fairly still waters, with a good entry and exit point, and at a slow speed when crossing ponds or other water obstacles. Soldiers also got bonked in the head—thank goodness for helmets—by a dislodged hatch after hitting one of the many *damn-it* stumps in the swampy training areas. Having to repair the APCs often interrupted our field training exercises. I can only imagine the amount of money spent throughout the military for maintenance on APCs. Maintaining them took valuable time away from our training. Also, I frankly hated slogging through the swamps. Essentially, I had become increasingly discouraged. A little over a year into my tour of duty at Fort Stewart, I researched other opportunities in the U.S. Army and seriously considered submitting a formal request through my chain of command for a change of assignment.

The 2/34 INF Battalion Officers

Despite everything, I also had very positive aspects of my time at Fort Stewart. One was particularly important. I met, dated and began a relationship with Maria Caballero. Her father was also in the U.S. Army and stationed there. He was in one of the Field Artillery units. Maria and I actually met while I was shopping at the local Kmart store in Hinesville, the small town next to Fort Stewart. She worked at the customer service desk. I'd noticed her and smiled at her often, but hadn't yet talked to her. In fact, our first date was a result of one of my visits to Kmart. I remember seeing her at the customer desk when I entered the store, but somehow she was the cashier when it was time for me to check out and pay. Maria and I talked about some of my items, including a can of racquet balls. During our brief conversation, she led me to believe she played racquetball. I asked if I could set up a game together on the following Saturday and she agreed. So our first date was a racquetball game at one of the gyms on base.

I picked her up and we were both excited to spend some time together. After we got on the court and warmed up, I served the ball against the front wall and expected Maria to return the serve. The ball never came back. I turned around and Maria had a sheepish grin on her face. She had no idea how to play racquetball. I quickly realized what had just happened. I smiled, walked over to her and gave her a kiss. She'd tricked me and we both had a good laugh about it. We talked for the next hour or two, and got to know one another better. She told me that at first her family was skeptical about her dating a soldier, but when she told her parents I was an officer, they seemed to warm up about me. From that point on we had several more dates, going to the movies, having dinners, and visiting Savannah. Unfortunately, a few months later Maria's father got orders for a new assignment. Maria, her parents, and her four younger siblings were soon moving to Germany. Maria and I didn't know how this would impact our relationship, but we agreed to stay in touch, even if it meant we would be far apart from one another. We promised to send each other lots of letters and exchange phone calls. A long distance relationship was not ideal for either one of us, but soon another timely change helped our situation.

After much thought and research about different options, I submitted a formal request through my chain of command—all the way to the Pentagon—for a more challenging assignment. I wanted to join the Special Forces, more commonly known as the Green Berets. Though not everyone above me endorsed my request, my paperwork was still forwarded to the final decision-makers at the Department of the Army (DA) in Washington DC. My timing must have been good because within a few weeks my request for a change of assignment was approved. I soon received new orders.

My request and DA's approval did not please each of my bosses. In fact, my Battalion Commander, who was my Company Commander's boss, wanted to speak with me about my decision and intention. After knocking twice on his door he called me into his office with a very audible *"come"*. I stood at attention and properly reported to him saying, *"Sir, Lieutenant Williams reporting as ordered"*. He returned my salute and stepped

Eddie's Department of the Army (DA) photo

127

from behind his desk. Standing right in front of me and with one of those *looks* on his face, he berated me for several minutes about my desire to leave his command and his battalion. He informed me, using very colorful and direct language, how I was ruining my military career. He was also a West Pointer and had graduated fifteen years before me. He was a senior officer with the rank of Lieutenant Colonel and a Vietnam War veteran. In his opinion, the U.S. Army had made a significant investment in me, via West Point and several other military schools. He also mentioned that I had very good evaluations, had a good reputation as one of his junior officers, but was making a bad decision to become a *"snake eater"* (a common nickname for a Green Beret). I found out later that he had not endorsed my request when it was originally submitted a few weeks before. But since DA approved it anyway, he had essentially been overruled by decision-makers above his head at the Pentagon. He wasn't happy about it, so this was his way of letting me know. Recall my earlier comments that there are people in our lives who are less than supportive, maybe even negative about our desire to get out of our comfort zone and achieve our goals. His concern for me may have been sincere, and he probably had good intentions in looking after my career as one of his junior officers, but those above his head were looking out for the greater good and needs of the U.S. Army. He couldn't do anything to change DA's decision, but wanted to take his pound of flesh anyway. I almost felt that I was back at West Point being grilled by an upperclassman.

As I continued to stand at attention while he shared his opinion on my desire to leave, I thought for a few seconds about reconsidering my decision. But, I was not going to let him deter me from my desire to meet new challenges. My mind was made up and DA had approved it. His harsh criticism of my request for a new assignment was officially outweighed by the Pentagon's decision and new orders. I was soon on my way to attend the

U.S. Army Special Forces Qualification Course (SFQC) at Ft. Bragg, North Carolina.

My new challenge was to become a Green Beret. If I survived that very intense course, I would join the ranks of the world's most respected, highly trained, and elite soldiers. Their official title is U.S. Army Special Forces (SF). Green Berets work together in twelve-men Operational Detachments (also called "A-Teams"). Each member of the team has a specific job and cross train within the team, in order to be familiar with one another's job. The ranking officer is the team leader (Captain), with a second in command (Lieutenant or Warrant Officer), and ten highly skilled NCO's who specialize in operations, intelligence, weapons, communications, and medical functions. A twelve man A-team can take lives as quickly as save them. There is a saying about SF, *it may seem crazy to send only 12 guys into a hostile country, but it's not crazy when they are Special Forces.*

SF soldiers are elite because they can conduct several different types of missions all over the world*, Counterterrorism (CT), Direct Action (DA), Foreign Internal Defense (FID), Special Reconnaissance (SR), and Unconventional Warfare (UW)*. My desire to become a Green Beret and complete the arduous five-month course at Fort Bragg had me embark on an even more daunting challenge.

Fort Bragg is the home of the famous 82ⁿᵈ Airborne Division and other elite U.S. Army Commands such as the 18ᵗʰ Airborne Corps, John F. Kennedy Special Warfare Center (JFKSWC) and Special Operation Command (SOCOM). When I reported there, I was part of a SF training class of soldiers who'd come from various U.S. Army units all over the world. Like me, they

---

* See Missions of Special Forces in Appendix 2.

wanted to become the best of the best. I was both intimidated and impressed by the SF instructors, who seemed brash and confident, yet determined to build us up physically and mentally into capable SF officers, NCOs, and soldiers. They wore their green berets—the coveted symbol of their elite status—and I wanted to soon earn that same privilege. Though I was confident in my abilities to complete the course, I was nervous about whether I was mentally and physically able to survive the grueling training.

SFQC was mentally tough because of the quantity of material we had to learn. We conducted in-depth analysis of many nations, learning about their governmental and military structures, cultural norms, religions, geography, topography, infrastructure, and even dissected any potential terroristic sub-cultures.

We had in-depth discussions about how to conduct overt and covert Special Forces operations within each country. We learned and applied small unit planning and tactics, medical, weapons, and communication training. These were important because Special Forces are tasked to teach a variety of skills when deployed, such as; first aid, water purification, digging wells, cultivating farm fields, building structures, roads, bridges, and teaching our allies how to become self-sufficient and defend themselves against their enemies. This required a keen knowledge of each respective country.

SFQC was physically demanding because it included day and night activities, airborne operations (parachute jumps with and without equipment), land navigation using map & compass, long grueling timed marches carrying heavy military back packs (called ruck sacks), hand-to-hand combat training, in-depth operational planning, and effectively doing this with limited sleep and food.

We also had officers from U.S. allied countries in our class which added an additional dimension to our training. Several of the allied officers discussed their respective country's governmental structure and unclassified military operations and capabilities. This reinforced the importance of our relationships and joint training needs. We learned a lot of first-hand information about their allies, enemies, and perspectives on conducting military operations. We also got to know one another on a social level. Each of the U.S. Officers was partnered with an Allied Officer to help mentor and administratively assist them during the course. My Allied Officer colleague was from Thailand and very proud to represent his country in the SFQC course. He was also very attentive to the course material, physically fit, and motivated to complete the course. He and I got along very well. During our off-duty time we talked about our families, backgrounds, and interests. He also introduced me to Thai food and customs. I'll

With SF colleagues at break during SFQC field training

never forget when he invited me to his room where he and a fellow Thai officer cooked some traditional Thai meals on a portable burner. This wasn't allowed but I thought it best not to create an international incident, so long as they didn't burn down the building. I enjoyed the food until I bit into one of the extremely hot peppers he'd added for seasoning. My mouth was under the faucet for at least five minutes, while my two Thai colleagues rolled on the floor in laughter. Other Allied Officers were from the Philippines, South Korea, Malawi, Israel and other countries.

After the arduous physical and mental training, graduation from the SFQC was another proud day in my military career and life. I'd earned the privilege to wear the Green Beret, and put the Special Forces tab on my uniform. I was soon assigned to one of the Special Forces Groups. Each Special Forces Group align their training, missions, and forces to specific geographic areas of operations (AO's) around the world; the Far East/Asia, Europe/Eastern Europe, Middle East, Central & South America, or Africa. Shortly before graduation, I received orders assigning me to 1st Battalion, 10th Special Forces Group (Airborne) located in southern Germany. This made me extremely happy for a

Graduation from the Special Forces Qualification Course (SFQC) at Fort Bragg, NC. Eddie, back row on right. In front me is my Thai Officer colleague

couple of reasons. I would soon be stationed in the country of my mother's family heritage. More importantly, I was going to be much closer to Maria.

As a Special Forces Officer, I was again responsible for the welfare, training, and morale of soldiers. But this time, I was among a much more select and elite group of seasoned soldiers. During my time in the 1st Bn/10th SFG(A), we trained and conducted joint operations with several military forces including Germany, England, Belgium, Luxembourg, and Norway. These joint U.S.-Allied exercises were important in order to gain experience working together, develop relationships, understand one another's capabilities, and build camaraderie. We also conducted in-depth studies of the people, languages, cultures, terrain and infra-structure within our specific area of operation (AO).

Each A-team prepared to infiltrate their respective AO's using parachutes (low altitude), scuba dive, skydive (high altitude), ski, or even walk into them. The objective was to link up with friendly forces in our AO and then conduct the team-specific mission. An historic example of this occurred during WWII when the American Office of Strategic Services (the OSS was the predecessor of Special Forces) worked with the French Resistance and fought the German Army in occupied France. SF also faught in the European and Pacific Theaters. Special Forces also operated extensively throughout Southeast Asia during the Vietnam War. A more recent

Special Forces soldiers on horseback in Afghanistan

example were Special Forces who rode on horseback during the early stages of the Afghanistan war. Those SF grew beards and dressed in Afghan clothing, to blend in and deploy with the Afghan military in order to help U.S.-friendly tribal forces against the Taliban and other insurgents. Many of them spoke the language, various dialects, and studied Afghanistan in-depth before they deployed.

I was initially assigned as the Executive Officer (second in charge) of Special Forces A-team ODA-036. I learned a great deal from the experienced and elite soldiers on the team. We continuously trained to deploy and operate in several types of environments. Our training included; parachute jumping, snow and cross-country skiing, mountain climbing, water infiltration techniques, along with various weapons, winter warfare, and survival training. As a result, I was in top physical shape and peak endurance. Though the training was intense, I also took time off to rest and relax. Maria and I stayed in contact and since she was only a few hours away, I visited her often.

Maria's family lived in the town of Wiesbaden in northern Germany. I was stationed in the southern German town of Bad Toelz. Though we called one another often, we also took the train or drove the autobahn (German highway) to visit one another. Our relationship blossomed and grew more serious just at a time when I needed her care and attention the most.

My A-team conducted several detailed planning sessions (called *isolation*) for major training exercises. A couple of them were called *Flintlock* and *Reforger*. During one isolation session, we planned a mission in one country then flew over and parachuted into another country—as if jumping behind enemy lines—to link up with friendly troops and jointly conduct our mission. We were to be self-sufficient, which meant parachuting in with the equipment and supplies needed for several days—or until we were resupplied by air drops. We'd planned a night jump into pitch black darkness from the ramp of a U.S. Air Force C-130 aircraft at about eight hundred feet above the ground. This height gave us just enough time for the parachute to open, then release and lower the equipment from our harnesses and land safely. The primary drop zone was a farmer's field that had been surveyed and approved by our Company and Battalion operations staff the day before our infiltration. Unfortunately, the farmer must have plowed the field during the day just before our jump. After several days of isolation, we conducted an extensive briefback; where the entire team and each team member thoroughly presented all mission essential details, individual functions, and numerous contingencies to our commanders and staff. All of our mission information had been thoroughly rehearsed and memorized during isolation. Once our commanders and staff were confident we had effectively planned our mission and could execute it, we were ready to go.

During the infiltration flight I was excited about my role and the team's ability to conduct the mission. As we jumped into the moonless night, we were actually dropped from an altitude slightly lower than we'd planned. It was so dark that I could only see the glow sticks attached to our equipment as we descended. After my parachute opened and just before I was able to release and lower the extra ninety-five pounds of equipment attached to my harness, I hit the ground. I landed extremely hard on my left side and on one of the newly plowed furrows of the farm field. My left ankle broke because of the hard impact of the combined weight of me, my own equipment, and the extra equipment I jumped in with. I knew I'd gotten hurt as soon as I hit the ground, but remained still for a few seconds. I did a quick assessment of my condition and even tried to put some weight on my left leg. It didn't work!

ODA-036 just before our mission and my "bad" landing

Fortunately, I landed near my team's Junior Medic, Staff Sergeant Gary Jones, who'd heard the pop when my ankle broke. He quickly got out of his parachute harness and crawled over to me. I whispered to him, *"My left leg isn't supposed to look like this!"* He agreed and confirmed that I had indeed broken my ankle—and broken it badly. He immediately injected my left thigh with a syringe of morphine to dull the pain. We then linked up with our in-country friendlies, and quickly initiated our contingency plans to continue the mission. As I was carried off the drop zone to get further medical attention, I discovered that two other team members were also injured during the infiltration. One had a broken leg and the other a badly sprained knee. Three other soldiers from other teams jumping in that night were also injured. Two had sprained ankles and one had both a sprained ankle and torn meniscus. That night turned out to be very bad for our SF teams.

Special Forces team members *cross train* to learn one another's jobs for just this sort of situation; should someone get injured or the mission require the team to split into three-man or six-man sub-teams. With three of us injured the remainder of the team continued the mission. In the middle of the night, the three of us were taken to a local medical clinic for treatment. The medical staff used ether to put me under before they reset my broken and severely dislocated left ankle. We were soon medevac'd by helicopter to a full-service hospital. There I finally had time to think about everything that had just occurred over the previous few hours and the seriousness of my situation. Though I was heavily medicated, I saw the severity of my injury both on the X-rays and displayed on the doctor's faces. I heard seriousness in their voices as they gave me their initial diagnosis and prognosis.

The doctors wanted to immediately fuse my ankle because it was so badly broken. As I contemplated their dire words I was very worried and shocked. Clearly, this would instantly end my participation in Special Forces and probably end my military career. I practically begged them for other options. After several minutes talking with me and then among themselves, the doctors made their decision. Because of my young age and very good physical condition, they opted to take an interim step. They would insert a three-inch screw into my ankle and allow it to heal over the next few months. Then they would re-evaluate my situation to determine a long term approach.

I was sent home to rest and ordered to keep my ankle elevated and immobile. They told me I could not put any weight on it for the next few months because this initial period of time was critical in the healing process. Within the ankle is a small hour-glass shaped bone called the talus. I had broken it at the thinnest (and weakest) point and it was critical that I allow it to heal. Before discharging me, they reinforced their instructions and reminded me that fusing my ankle was not yet out of the question.

When I got to my apartment (bachelor officer quarters or BOQ) I called Maria and told her about my broken ankle and situation. She immediately took the train to visit me. I couldn't get around easily and certainly couldn't drive. One of my friends picked her up at the Bad Toelz train station. I was thrilled to see her. She made several trips back and forth to keep me company during the next several months. After the initial two months, I had the follow up appointment with the doctors. The X-rays showed my ankle was healing well. They opted to take the screw out, let the entire talus bone fully heal over another few months and then re-evaluate again. I still couldn't put any weight on it. It took several more months before they felt confident with their decision not to fuse my ankle. The medical record narrative summary (clinical resume) stated:

PRESENT ILLNESS: Pain in left ankle

HISTORY OF PRESENT ILLNESS: Sustained injury to the left ankle during night parachute jump. He was taken to a civilian hospital where the facture-dislocation was reduced under general anesthesia.

PHYSICAL EXAMINATION: This 24 year old white male, was comfortable in splint. Toes warm and move freely. X-rays: short fracture of neck of talus and calcaneus. Initial films reveal sub-talar dislocation. He was taken to the operating room with an open reduction over the fracture of the talus performed in fixation with the screw. He was kept in a splint. He was doing well post operatively. He was give short leg cast. He did well. It is much better but it is not good. Bone scan was then at one month and suggested vascularity well healed.

DIAGNOSIS: Fracture dislocation of the left talus, reduced, with fractured of talus.

PROCEDURE: Open reduction internal fixation with the bone grafts to the talus.

SPECIAL PROCEDURE: Bone scan

They also told me that even though my talus bone would structurally heal, I would always have some discomfort with my ankle. They were also concerned about the blood circulation in my ankle and foot, and told me that I would probably have arthritis in it for the rest of my life. Before releasing me to go back home they gave me strict rehabilitation guidelines which I followed to the letter.

My ankle took an entire year to heal. Within that timeframe I had several hard plaster non-weight bearing casts. After more re-evaluations, the doctors gave me permission to put weight on my left ankle to regain strength and mobility in the ankle, left leg and muscles. Then, I had several walking casts, with a piece of rubber on the bottom to help absorb the shock of putting weight on my left leg. After those casts, I was allowed to use an ankle brace and endure an extensive physical therapy regimen. One rehab technique was to stand waist-deep in the swimming pool for buoyancy and take my weight off the ankle. With my left foot on the pool floor, I'd raise and lower the heel of my left foot to gradually regain full range of motion in my ankle. This exercise was very painful but worked after several months of repetition.

Throughout my year of recuperation, Maria and I spent a lot of time together. She would take the train to visit me in Bad Toelz, or I would drive or take the train to visit her in Wiesbaden. We took long walks together to help with the rehabilitation, but also for us to just talk. As a result of all of our time together, our relationship blossomed even more and we fell in love. We had long conversations about our families, interests, hopes and dreams. We had a lot in common and really enjoyed each other's company. I appreciated how she looked after me. She encouraged me through the painful rehab exercises. We also went on some of the traditional German Volksmarches in the beautiful German countryside. During one of my visits to Wiesbaden, I asked Maria's father permission to marry her. I was very nervous about talking with him, but relieved when our conversation went well and he gave me his blessing to marry Maria. Over the next few weeks I planned for the right time to propose. Interestingly, as my dad had done many years before, I formally requested permission from my commander to marry Maria. He approved! On my next

Maria and Eddie, civil ceremony wedding at town hall in Bad Toelz, Germany. Alongside are Justice of the Peace and Translator

visit to Wiesbaden a few weeks later, Maria and I had a dinner date in a very nice restaurant. At a point in our conversation that I knew was the right moment, I asked Maria to marry me. I felt confident our relationship was strong and she would accept my proposal but was still very anxious. She hesitated just long enough to make me sweat for a few seconds. When she said *"yes"* I was relieved, thrilled, and grateful that Maria and I would soon be together as husband and wife. We quickly drove back to her family's apartment to announce and celebrate our engagement. Throughout this time my parents were well aware of our growing relationship and my love for Maria. I called them that night to share the good news. They were thrilled.

Maria and I were actually married twice while we lived in Germany. We had a traditional German civil ceremony officiated by the local German Justice of the Peace in Bad Toelz that October. A fellow SF officer, good friend, and West Point classmate and his wife, Tim and Sunghee Sherwood, were our witnesses.

Maria also promised her mother that we would have a family ceremony. After a lot of planning and coordination we had a formal religious ceremony in Wiesbaden the following April. We had a minister marry us in the presence of lots of family and friends. My boss and close friend, Pete Dillon, was my best man. Pete's wife, Fran was Maria's matron-of-honor, and Maria's sister, Iris Caballero, was her maid-of-honor. Another very close friend Lorraine Sinnigen, was a bride's-maid. It was really special to have her there, because her husband Tim, a fellow SF officer and close friend was deployed with his A-Team on a very sensitive international mission at the time.

We had the ceremony in a public park in the center of Wiesbaden on a beautiful spring day. In fact, since our ceremony was in a public park, some of the people who were walking by stopped to watch it. Before we left for the reception, a German by-stander asked one of our guests if we were Hawaiian because our ceremony was being held outdoors. At the reception, Maria and I heard about the comment and had a good laugh.

Maria and Eddie formal wedding
in Wiesbaden, Germany

Maria and I had known one another for about two and a half years before we were married. We'd grown very close during that time and had already experienced a lot together since we'd first met in Georgia. It was so interesting how things had worked out as our relationship matured. Our wedding day was wonderful. We spent our honeymoon in Austria, and then looked forward to our future together and the challenges we would face together.

We were able to move from my BOQ just outside Flint Kaserne (the German name of our military base). Interestingly, the Kaserne had previously been a German-SS officer training school during WWII. We were assigned to a family apartment inside the Kaserne. This was also around the time of my final ankle evaluation. The doctors told me that my left ankle had fully structurally healed and gave me permission to return to normal duty. Yet, their definition of normal duty was not *normal Special Forces duty*. During the first few months, I purposely demonstrated to my superiors that I was indeed ready for duty.

I participated in several strenuous runs during our morning physical fitness training sessions, and made sure I did well during mandatory timed endurance walks with a heavy rucksack. A few months later, I was given the command of my own Special Forces Operational Detachment A-Team, ODA-011. The real test of my ankle's recovery occurred literally one year to the day after I'd broken it. I conducted a parachute jump—this time without equipment, called a *Hollywood jump*—to confirm my confidence and verify that my ankle would handle the impact of landing. Candidly, I was extremely nervous as I jumped from the helicopter and descended to the ground. I landed fine and conducted a perfect parachute landing fall (PLF – the proper way of landing and allowing the fleshy portions of the body to absorb the jolting impact). After I gathered my parachute and walked off the drop zone, I was thrilled at being able to jump again. I was proud of myself for having endured all the rehab necessary over the past year, to return to duty and rejoin my SF brothers.

For the next two years I validated my physical abilities and leadership skills in my position as Team Leader of ODA-011. My team was composed of very capable and dedicated SF soldiers. My Team Sergeant, Master Sergeant (MSG) Larry Martens, who we call "Gpa" (short for grandpa because he was the oldest member of the team) and I got along extremely well. After he and I discussed our team's training objectives and finalized the training schedules, I knew he would prepare the team and delegate responsibilities, so we were ready for whatever mission, exercise, or training activities we needed to perform. Though he is now a retired Sergeant Major (SGM) he and I still stay in touch. I also stay connected with other ODA-011 team members. Life-long bonds are typically formed among SF soldiers because of all they endure together.

I conducted a variety of training exercises with my team. This included, parachute jumps with and without equipment, running many miles, hiking numerous mountain trails, and conducting rugged and stressful endurance activities. Though my left ankle held up well, I knew in the back of my mind that though it had *healed*—to the extent the talus bone had mended—I was often reminded it was not as strong as it used to be. Just as the doctors had told me during my recuperation period, there were several times when my ankle was stiff and sore, became swollen, and acted like a weather barometer. The aches gave me advanced warning of approaching rain, snow, and bad weather. Though it had medically healed, I began to realize I could no longer fully endure all of the activities required of Special Forces for the rest of my career. Candidly, ever since the doctors had cleared me to return to full duty, I consciously favored my left ankle. During parachute jumps I would land on my right side whenever possible. When hiking rugged or uneven terrain, I'd compensate by stepping up with my right foot first. Before strenuous rucksack marches, long runs, and other physical training activities, I'd tightly wrap my left ankle for additional support. I was essentially prolonging the inevitable question. How long would my left ankle hold out?

Eddie (back row middle) with his SF A-team, ODA-011

Before my pitch dark parachute jump (with equipment) which ended with a broken left ankle, I had sustained no major injuries while enduring numerous physical challenges throughout my military career. They included the physical and athletic activities at West Point, several U.S. Army schools, my first assignment at Fort Stewart, and my SF assignment. Had my good fortune run out? Every time my ankle ached or became swollen, it prompted me to ask myself whether I'd reached a physical plateau in my military career, as an officer, and as a Green Beret. I was no longer in peak condition or top physical capability. Though my left ankle had mended, it didn't have the same strength, especially having broken it in the thinnest part of the hour-glass shaped talus bone. Lots of other questions crossed my mind. Would my ankle hold for another fifty or one hundred parachute jumps and landings? How many more miles of grueling endurance marches with heavy rucksack loads would it endure? Would it be strong enough to support me during the numerous other physical challenges that were still ahead in a demanding Special Forces career?

More importantly, I didn't want to risk the lives of my SF team if I couldn't hold my own, during future SF training exercises or potential combat missions. As ODA-011 Team Leader, I certainly didn't want my soldiers doing anything—especially any kind of physical activity—that I couldn't excel. I was accustomed to setting the example. If I couldn't score the maximum on physical fitness tests or endurance activities, I would no longer be the leader I wanted to be and was expected to be for my team. I didn't want to put my team at risk, especially if my ankle broke again. This reality diminished my self-confidence and forced me to consider difficult questions. Would my mended ankle jeopardize my ability to remain in Special Forces? If not, would I then be satisfied transferring to a non-Special Forces assignment, or remain in Special Forces in some other non-operational or non-deployable job? Even if such a position existed, would I be satisfied with it for the remainder of my career? Was my ankle injury a not-very-subtle signal that it was time for me to move on and into another career? Over the next few months Maria and I had long conversations about all of these issues. We talked about our future in the U.S. Army and my future in Special Forces.

There were several other contributing factors, besides my ankle, that Maria and I discussed regarding our future. One was the inherent nature of Special Forces. SF are expected to focus on the mission, which frequently required long deployments without the ability to tell spouses or family members critical details; where we're going, what we're doing or going to do, and when we're expected to return. It was widely known in the military, that many marriages among Special Forces soldiers typically become lifeless unions. Couples stay together only because military spouses are too busy during deployments—looking after their children and managing family business—to file for divorce. Maria and I had already seen examples of this among several of our fellow officer and NCO colleagues in our Special Forces Battalion.

Additionally, Maria and I were aware of and personally witnessed some of the *politics* within the military and SF. Candidly, we didn't like it. When I was single, I focused on being an effective and dedicated officer by applying my skills to further my career as a leader of Infantry and then SF soldiers. Now that I was married I had to focus not just on what was good for me and my future, but what was good for both Maria and me. It was our future not just my future.

We witnessed several incidents where fellow officers conducted themselves badly in both public and private situations. One of the senior officers in my chain of command, a full Colonel, was caught illegally trafficking and selling weapons. After his court martial, he served a lengthy prison sentence. He certainly wasn't setting the example for us to emulate such behavior. On another occasion, a Colonel publicly embarrassed our German hosts and co-workers by berating the quality of German appliances and discouraged all American soldiers and their families from using them. I also witnessed one of my immediate senior SF officers ruin the career of a fellow junior officer because of an incident in poor judgment. There was no doubt the junior officer had made a mistake. Rather than use the situation as a teachable moment for professional development, my SF Battalion Commander chose to end his career. Though other options seemed more appropriate, many of us were disappointed with how our boss handled the situation in such a drastic manner.

Maria and I also knew that several officers and NCOs had affairs and were wife-swapping. I also knew that non-Special Forces officers were *pulling rank* (using their senior rank to influence lower ranking soldiers) in situations with Special Forces soldiers or belittling their spouses. Candidly, some of these officers were SF *wanna-bees*; meaning that they couldn't or didn't make it into Special Forces and were going to get even. In fact, one of my Team NCO's asked for my help with a situation involving his wife. She had an administrative job for a non-SF officer, and felt threatened by her boss when she couldn't work overtime hours. Also, she wasn't allowed to take time off at the same time her husband had time off, in-between our scheduled training exercises. They didn't know how to handle the dilemma and sought my help. I spoke with the officer and his boss. Though the situation seemed resolved, I felt that there would still be a backlash against my NCO's wife. Maria and I were personally involved in another situation, when an officer who outranked me made a big deal when he discovered that our quarters (apartment) was larger than his. He actually approached me and demanded that we switch quarters. It didn't happen. The *politics* of the military was also exemplified when an African-American Congressmen came to Germany to visit a few of the units stationed there. The senior Commander of Flint Kaserne insisted that Maria and I attend a dinner, so the Congressman could talk with a black SF officer and his wife. Though there were only two black SF Officer's in our Battalion of fifty officers, this situation was glaringly politically motivated. The Congressman knew it. Maria and I knew it. To the Congressman's credit he was cordial and never brought it up. Some of these situations were petty while others were very serious. Collectively, they added to the thought process and discussions Maria and I were having about our future.

By the way, it bears mention that during my time in 1/10th Special Forces Battalion, my skin color never seemed to be an issue. Leadership, drive, physical aptitude, decision-making, and the ability to work together as a team were the hallmarks of every SF Officer and NCO. We trained together, jumped together, lived together, and when the mission called for it, deployed together. It was irrelevant whether the SF soldier was black, white, blue, green, stood six-foot five or five-foot three, had blond hair, or no hair.

Ultimately, Maria and I questioned whether we wanted to deal with the *politics* we witnessed on a regular basis for the rest of our career in SF. I neared re-assignment to attend upper level officer schooling, other assignments, and consideration for promotion to the rank of Major. Based on my evaluations and performance, I was confident I would be promoted soon. We also knew my future assignments would include both staff and command jobs, and that *politics* would probably play an even greater role in our future. We had to seriously evaluate our willingness to deal with it and whether the excitement and adventure of those future assignments and locations would outweigh the inevitable *politics*.

We had to soon make a serious decision whether to stay in SF or leave the military entirely. Up to that point in my military career, I'd had an extremely rewarding time being involved in many exciting military experiences and leading some of the finest soldiers in the U.S. Army. During our time in Germany, Maria and I made many life-long friendships. We also enjoyed the opportunity to visit several wonderful countries while on leave, including trips to Austria, Spain, France, Italy, and a Holy Land tour in Israel. Additionally, I was well past my fifth year of active duty and had satisfied my five-year obligation after West Point.

Maria and I also discussed and shared our dilemma with trusted fellow officers and their wives. They gave us mixed feedback about the possibility of resigning my commission and leaving Special Forces. Recall, my earlier comments that sometimes those around us may not be supportive of our goals, ambitions or willingness to step out of our comfort zone. Some of our friends were supportive with whatever decision we made. Others gave us feedback like; *"How will you make a living?" "You don't know what it's like to be a civilian!" "You're not going to like it out there in the civilian*

Maria and Eddie during a German-American function at Bad Toelz, Germany

world." "You're a West Pointer, why give up a guaranteed career!"
"How are you going to translate being a Green Beret on a resume ...
experienced snake-eater for hire?" and *"Are you nuts?"*

Maria and I finally made a decision. As our tour in Germany
neared an end, and after considering all the pros and cons, we
decided it was time to move on. Together we were about to
face an entirely new challenge. We would leave the military and
become civilians. I signed and submitted the paperwork through
my chain-of-command to DA resigning my commission.

Some of my superiors were not pleased, and I informally heard
about their non-supportive comments. After two years of
A-Team command, I'd developed into one of the most respected
SF Team Leaders in our Battalion and in 10th SF Group. With
my resignation, I was almost instantly denigrated to near-traitor
status. To counter them, those fellow SF officers and NCO's
whose opinions I truly valued shook my hand, wished me
well, and saluted me a little crisper when they heard about my
resignation. They respected the extremely tough decision Maria
and I had made. During my last week on active duty, and to
personally leave with my head held high, I took the U.S. Army
Physical Fitness Test already scheduled for our Battalion. I was
getting out and didn't have to take the test, but did so anyway. I
achieved the maximum score of three-hundred points. Candidly,
I wanted to show my bosses, and more importantly my team
members and SF brothers, that I was leaving at the top of my
game. On the final weekend before Maria and I departed, our
close friends hosted a wonderful going-away dinner party for
us at the Leonhardi Keller, our favorite restaurant in Bad Toelz.
Several SF colleagues and German civilian friends gave us
farewell gifts, hugs, and wished us well. We fondly discussed our
time at Bad Toelz, our unit, mission, and the elite SF soldiers
who worked hard to prepare for known and unknown events. I

loved my time on my A-Team with my SF brothers. My team saw us off at the train station on that final morning. Even elite SF soldiers cry and hug one another when we end close working relationships. Our friendships would last forever.

Our colleague's comments were quite accurate. Maria and I didn't know how to be civilians. We'd both grown up as Army-brats. I'd gone to West Point straight from high school and then into the military. Maria was the daughter of an NCO and then an SF officer's wife. Neither of us had jobs after we left the U.S. Army. We didn't know how my experience in the Infantry and Special Forces would translate into the civilian workplace. Without exaggeration, we were scared, nervous, worried and excited about the unknown. We had no idea what lay ahead for us. That said, we had each other and would face the unknown future together.

CHAPTER 11

The Path Train to World Trade Center

"You must be the change you wish to see in the world."

~ Gandhi

My new job was to find ... a new job! Maria and I immediately focused on the task of how to transition from the military to civilian life. To prepare I contacted an organization that recruited junior military officers (JMO's). The company, Military Recruiting Institute (MRI), specialized in finding civilian jobs for young officers leaving all branches of the military. MRI provided me information about companies looking to hire JMO's, and helped me translate my military skills and experience into a civilian-friendly resume for hiring managers. They also coordinated informational meetings for groups of JMO's and scheduled interviews when we got back to the states. There was an extensive market for JMO's in civilian positions such as, plant managers, management trainees, and entry-level sales reps. Corporations recognized JMO's important skill sets. They are experienced supervisors, mission oriented, calm under pressure and stress, independent thinkers, self-motivated, small unit leaders, and have the critical aspects of attention-to-detail, planning, and a strong work ethic. Corporations look to hire JMOs because they bring a foundational level of skills and the proven ability to quickly learn new skills and concepts. JMO's enter the civilian workforce with identifiable and transferable skills, often proven through real world situations, which can directly enhance an organization's productivity. JMO's can adapt to new training and policies of their new civilian employers.

I shared all of this information and several potential opportunities with Maria to calm her nervousness and assure her that we would be fine. Inwardly, I was a wreck about our uncertain future. We were transitioning from the military environment where we knew all the rules, policies, regulations and requirements. The military gave us a guaranteed pay check every two weeks. We had a place to live, a job, a specific job description, an expectation of promotion, advancement, and continuing education. Maria and I also had medical and dental care, vacation time, and several other benefits. As we entered the civilian world, each of those critical items was neither guaranteed nor certain. Clearly, I had to quickly and confidently show her we made the right decision to get out and travel down an entirely new path.

When we returned to the states, we took a couple of months to transition and adjust to being civilians. We traveled across the country visiting family on both coasts and several friends along the way. I was on *terminal leave*. I'd accumulated two months of vacation time prior to resigning and continue to get paid. Then I was off the military payroll and totally on my own. MRI had me complete dozens of job applications and several interviews. But, three months after my pay ended, I had not landed a job and we were concerned. We lived on savings and decided to stay with Maria's parents. Her father had retired in Fayetteville, North Carolina about a year before I'd resigned. We were also near the familiar military base of Fort Bragg. At about the time Maria and I were extremely anxious about our situation, I got a call from MRI. One of the companies extended me a job offer. After confirming the position, salary, benefits, and start day, I had landed my first civilian job. Maria and I were absolutely thrilled and relieved. It was an entry-level sales position as a Group Insurance Sales Representative (Group Rep) with the Prudential Insurance Company of America. The position required me to sell a broad variety of employee benefits products to employers throughout New Jersey and in New York City. We celebrated by having a very nice dinner with Maria's parents, to also show our appreciation for their support and hospitality. Maria and I packed our car and set out for our new adventure in New Jersey.

Prudential put me through an extensive six-month training program, called the Group Rep Orientation Course (GROC). The training included; sales techniques, insurance underwriting, customer service, and details on the broad variety of Prudential's group insurance products; medical, dental, group life insurance and disability plans. I also took the state insurance license exam.

Eddie and Maria visit with Mom and Dad in CA

Maria and I lived in Morristown, New Jersey, about an hour west of New York City. The Prudential sales office was a thirty-minute drive from our one-bedroom apartment. Though we only had one car our commute situation turned out to be very convenient. As we were settling in and running errands, Maria went into the bank just across the street from our apartment complex to get a job application. After a brief conversation with the branch manager Maria was asked to stay for a formal interview. Maria got a job as a bank teller that day, partly because she was bi-lingual (English and Spanish), had experience working as a bank teller in the American Express Bank while we were stationed in Germany, and was in the right place at the right time.

I enjoyed working for Prudential and did well. I liked calling on corporate clients, meeting with customers, working with insurance brokers, negotiating benefits packages, and servicing several accounts all over New Jersey and a few in New York City. Many of the skills I'd learned in the military like public speaking and tailoring presentations to the specific audience were very applicable in my new sales job. Other military skills such as showing up on time, being prepared, and wearing the correct uniform (typically a suit) also came in handy. I explained benefit plan costs and details, conducted employee enrollment meetings, and managed Q&A sessions. I also had to effectively multi-task. This involved designing competitive and profitable proposals my underwriters would support, while simultaneously incenting insurance brokers to promote my products through fair commissions. I also had to meet our office's sales objectives and generate my own bonuses. My military experience in building relationships certainly came in handy. My job involved working with a variety of clients, insurance consultants, fellow group reps, account executives, prospects, and co-workers from many departments in our regional office.

My job also provided some very memorable personal experiences. One of my accounts was a shipping company located in One World Trade Center (WTC) in New York City. I conducted service calls with them a few times each year to ensure their benefits plan was going smoothly. This also included explaining the benefits package to newly hired employees, and help employees get claims paid or new insurance cards. I rarely drove into NYC because the commuter traffic was terrible. I used public transportation, either the New Jersey Transit bus or the PATH train. The bus ride took longer than the train, but since I wasn't driving I had more time to review the client file and better prepare for the visit. Each visit to the World Trade Center was a thrill. I caught the PATH train in Newark, which went under the Hudson River and ended under the World Trade Center Complex in NYC. As the PATH train doors opened a flood of people exited, then went up at least twenty banks of escalators into the massive buildings. Thousands of people worked in the WTC complex. It was a small city. On one visit I'd somehow forgotten my belt. The WTC ground floor was a mall-like series of shops, stores and restaurants. I easily bought another one before my meeting. The account was located so high up that it was often difficult to concentrate during my meetings, because the view of the New York Bay, Bridges, and Statue of Liberty was stunning.

Eddie (2nd row, 4th from right) in the Prudential Group Rep Training class

Another client was a foreign airline whose NYC office was on 5th Avenue. For those visits I took the NJ Transit bus to the Port Authority. Those visits were interesting adventures too. The Port Authority was a place where all sorts of people hung out including the homeless, drunks, prostitutes, day laborers, drug dealers, peddlers, three-card-monte hustlers, tourists, people in-transit, and anyone who had nowhere else to be. I had a standard routine for those trips. As soon as the bus pulled into the Port Authority, I'd get off and immediately walk directly to the ticket window and purchase my return-trip ticket. I'd walk from the Port Authority to my client's office a few blocks away. At the end of the appointment, I could then go straight to and get on the return bus. I wouldn't have to stop for anything or anyone. The Port Authority was not only a transit spot in NYC, it was a slice of humanity. Though my trips there were always an adventure I spent only the time that was absolutely necessary.

Maria and I visited many of the tourist attractions; Ellis Island, the Statue of Liberty, South Street Sea Port, Rockefeller Plaza, 42nd Street, the storefront Christmas decorations on 5th Avenue, and several Broadway shows. Though we enjoyed ourselves, we felt—in general—that the people in the New Jersey and New York area were very aggressive and rude. But not rude in a personal way, just in how people interacted with one another. They drove fast, talked fast, and were impatient. They honked their horns if you didn't immediately move when the light turned green. They'd cut you off while driving. Even in restaurants and cafés, the wait staff seemed annoyed if you weren't immediately ready to order. I think people acted this way because the local lifestyle was fast-paced. We also found it very expensive to live in the NJ/NYC area. We researched real estate prices in hopes of buying a house and expanding our family. Even with our combined incomes we only found an affordable two-bedroom house several hours further east, almost in Pennsylvania. We settled for a two-bedroom apartment on the other side of our apartment complex. One day my boss—who was aware of my frustration with the high cost-of-living situation—approached me with an opportunity. He offered me a similar position with Prudential and a transfer to Atlanta, Georgia. I would sell similar Prudential group benefit products within the metro-Atlanta and north Georgia marketplace. Maria and I talked about the offer, made our decision quickly and coordinated the relocation package before the end of the week.

Moving again wasn't a big deal for either of us. Since we were both military brats, moving every couple of years was second nature. Having lived in Georgia a few years earlier, we jumped at the chance of going back and especially to Atlanta. In our opinion, the south was friendlier, had a lower cost-of-living, a slower pace of life and a more accommodating lifestyle. Shortly after we arrived, we found a four-bedroom house in the suburbs of northwest Atlanta. Our VA Loan allowed the monthly mortgage to be just slightly more than what we'd paid in rent for our two-bedroom apartment in New Jersey. After settling into our new home we looked forward to expanding our family.

Over the previous seven years Maria and I tried to have children, but weren't successful. Not having children was a huge void in our lives and marriage. This was another major challenge we were dealing with and wanted to overcome. We thought something was medically wrong with one or both of us, so we got checked out by our doctors. They told we would not be able to have kids the natural (or traditional) way. We then visited more doctors and specialists who suggested various options. One of them was in-vitro fertilization. With in-vitro, there were no guarantees, lots of medicines, tests, potential disappointments, and a great deal of expense. Maria and I talked with couples who had both succeeded and failed with in-vitro. They were candid about the physical and emotional toll they experienced and shared that the cost for each attempt was about $10,000. Maria and I were delighted for the couples who had children through in-vitro. After lots of discussion and prayer Maria and I decided not to pursue in-vitro. Our faith led us to believe that if it was God's will for us not to have kids the natural way, then we weren't supposed to tinker with the process. That was our personal perspective. Amazingly, just a short time later that decision was validated for us.

CHAPTER 12

A Very Diverse Family

"To add value to others, one must first value others."
~ *John C. Maxwell*

What happened next for Maria and I can only be explained as a testament of our faith. Shortly after we relocated to Atlanta, Maria attended and graduated from a technical school and became a surgical technician—also called a scrub nurse. She got a job working in the operating room of a hospital in Marietta, GA near where we lived. She prepared the operating rooms (O.R.) with appropriate equipment, surgical tools, instruments, and supplies. During the procedures, she would hand the instruments to the nurses and doctors and help manage the patients and O.R. resources.

She enjoyed her work and would occasionally share details about the life and death surgical procedures. After working in the O.R. for about five years she wanted a change of pace. Her options were to transfer to another department within the hospital or work in the office of one of the doctors from the O.R. Because of her skills, performance, and bilingual ability, she accepted a position in the hospital's Labor and Delivery (L&D) department. She transferred from the O.R. to L&D that August and looked forward to help women deliver their babies. This was both a wonderful opportunity and an ironic situation. Though we couldn't have children ourselves, Maria was going to help other women with this incredible miracle.

One day while Maria was at work in L&D, and I was conducting an employee benefits enrollment meeting for a client in Atlanta, she sent a message to my pager. I couldn't reply right away but glanced at it and recognized her work number. At a break I called her back. When she picked up the call, all she was able to say was, *"Guess what?"*

I replied, *"What?"*

She replied, *"Do you want a baby?"*

Confused, I replied, *"Excuse me?"*

She then repeated, *"Do you want a baby?"*

I answered, *"Sure!"*

She said, *"Well come over here and see our new son!"*

Obviously, I was anxious about what she meant but had to get back to my meeting. As soon as it ended, I called Maria back, got more details and then drove to the hospital. I met her at L&D. She explained the situation which had occurred earlier that morning.

A pregnant lady who was close to her due date, was driving back home to Cartersville, GA—about twenty minutes north of Marietta—after visiting her mother in Montgomery, AL. During her drive home she went into labor and barely made it to the emergency room of the hospital where Maria was working that day. Maria assisted the other staff nurses, a mid-wife and the doctor in the birthing room helping the lady deliver her baby boy. While Maria was cleaning the newborn and taking his footprints for the medical forms, she noticed the other nurses whispering to one another. When she had a chance to ask them what they were whispering about, they told her the mother wanted to give the baby up for adoption. The mother said she and her husband already had two children, and they simply could not afford another baby in their family. On the spot, Maria told the nurses, *"Okay, I'll keep the baby!"* Instantly, Maria realized she just assisted with the birth of the baby who was about to become our son. Frankly, it was incredible how the many connections in this situation came together. The birth mother had gone into labor while driving home and barely made it to the hospital. Maria had recently transferred to L&D and was working that day. Maria was assigned to that particular birthing room. The birth mother told the nurses about her willingness to allow her baby to be adopted. Maria's awareness and her confidence to speak up. No person could have orchestrated the timing of those events. Maria and I were obviously amazed, overjoyed, and excited at the opportunity to adopt the baby boy. We were also scared and totally unprepared for what had just occurred. From a practical standpoint, we had no baby clothes, no baby formula, no baby crib, and no baby anything. But we had friends, neighbors, and Walmart was open 24 hours. All of this was overwhelming but we were ready to deal with it.

Clearly, Maria and I had to go through the extensive formal adoption process. We didn't know any adoption lawyers. But the L&D nurses told Maria about a local law firm that could help. When we called their adoption attorney was busy with several other clients. He referred us to a colleague about two hours away in the north Georgia town of Blue Ridge. After a brief introductory phone conversation, the attorney, John Tucker, dropped what he was doing and drove straight to the hospital. He met separately with us and then with the birth mother. He explained to her the legal details related to giving her baby up for adoption and had her sign legal papers relinquishing parental rights. She didn't seem to have any issues with the process and provided some basic family medical history. Then, he explained to us the numerous steps required in Georgia to adopt the baby. We then agreed to meet again the next day at the hospital. Our attorney spent the night near the hospital preparing the paperwork. When we met the next morning, he had us sign legal papers and again clarified the steps of the adoption process. Essentially, after signing the documents he gave us legal authority to care for the baby during the state required ten-day waiting period. During that timeframe the birth parents could change their mind and we would have to return the baby. We had the choice to let the Georgia Department of Family and Children Services (DFACS) keep the baby for the ten-day period, but Maria and I chose to care for him instead. We paid the baby's hospital charges and John handed us our new son. We drove home with our new baby boy and prayed we would be able to keep him.

We exposed ourselves to a tremendous emotional risk. We were going to bond and care for him, knowing we might have to give him back at any time during the ten-day period. Each day was filled with anxiety and each night was sleepless. Our hearts stopped every time the phone rang. Maria and I trusted that this was all part of God's plan for us. We couldn't take our eyes off him and instantly bonded with him. We named him Matthew Evan Williams. By the way, Matthew means gift from God. We could breathe again when the ten-day period passed without incident. Legally, this meant that we had as much right to adopt him as his birth parents. The rest of the adoption process took several months. It involved lots of paperwork, background checks, DFACS interviews with our friends, employment verification, and an extensive in-house interview—more like an interrogation. Frankly, people who can have children naturally should go through this process. It was long and arduous. The court date for our adoption of Evan was a very happy day for everyone. The judge even said he looked forward to adoptions because they offset the many other unfortunate decisions he had to make in his court.

Evan was a beautiful baby. He had light brown skin like me. Passersby would often comment, *"He looks just like you dad!"* when we were at a store, mall, or park. Evan was my boy! Maria and I were overjoyed at becoming parents, something we didn't think was ever going to happen.

About sixteen months later, another baby was born near the hospital where Maria worked. But this baby was born at home and to a local high school student. She gave birth to a baby girl in her bathtub with the help of a high school girlfriend. Those young ladies didn't fully realize the danger of their situation. Apparently, the mother was bleeding so badly during the delivery that her girlfriend got scared and called 911. The EMT's brought the mother and her newborn baby girl to the emergency room.

During the previous months, Maria had mentioned to her colleagues and co-workers that we'd like to adopt another baby. Maria wasn't working in L&D that day, but her colleagues left her a message at the hospital's daycare center. Maria had dropped off Evan while running some errands nearby. When Maria picked him up she got the message and went straight to L&D. After she saw the baby, Maria called me on my cell phone. This time she said, *"Eddie, do you want to see your baby daughter? But she doesn't look like Evan."* I knew the drill by now and said, *"Sure, and I don't care what she looks like!"* I quickly went to L&D, found Maria and met our new daughter. We contacted the same adoption attorney who had helped us with Evan. He was eager to help us again. Again, he dropped what he was doing, drove to the hospital and separately spoke with us and the young mother. She was encouraged by her parents to give her baby girl up for adoption. After our lawyer got the legal papers signed, and explained the adoption process to everyone involved, we brought our daughter home. She was two days old. We now bonded with our baby girl. Evan didn't know what to make of the new addition to the family. He especially didn't like when she cried and all the attention she got. Again, Maria and I survived ten days of sleepless nights and nervous tension during the required waiting period. We named our daughter Madison Elise Williams. Maria liked the two names Madison and Elise, and I had no say in the matter.

Madison had Caucasian and Korean heritage. Her birth grandmother was native Korean. To complicate matters, our attorney discovered that Madison's birth father skipped town shortly after he found out that his girlfriend was pregnant. This required us to take a few additional steps in the adoption process. We had to subpoena the school system to get his last known address. For several weeks, we were required to place an adoption notice in both the local newspaper and the newspaper of the birth father's last known address, announcing our intent to adopt the baby. There was no reply to the notice, so we could move forward. Additionally, during our attorney's interview with the baby's birth family, he told us that Madison's birth mother never told her parents she was pregnant. They only found out when their daughter was at the emergency room after delivering the baby. It's amazing how this young woman could have hidden her pregnancy, but she must have hidden it very well.

As you can imagine, there are distinct heritage, complexion, and racial differences between Madison, Evan, Maria and me. We're a racially diverse family. In fact, if you think about it several continents are represented in our home. Maria is Puerto Rican, so as a *Latina*, she covers Central and South America. I'm German and African-American, which covers Europe and Africa. Evan is African-American too. Madison is Caucasian and Korean, which cover North America and Asia. We are a nice racial mix.

Maria and I were amazed with all that had occurred during the previous few years. We were blessed with two children, after thinking that having children was never going to happen. Equally interesting, I had grown up in a mixed-race family and now our kids would do the same. When reflecting on the process of adopting Evan and Madison, and the joy of raising them, I had to ask myself the obvious questions: how would my kids handle growing up in a mixed-race family? As mixed-race siblings would their experience be different from my experience? My answer could only be an unqualified—*absolutely!*

Evan and Madison would have their own unique experiences and memories as they grew up. Fortunately, many of the negative societal sentiments about mixed-race families and relationships that I'd experienced in the 1960's were not as relevant any longer. Fortunately, Evan and Madison were less likely

The Williams Family all dressed up at a family event

to encounter the same type of abuse and rudeness I'd endured as a kid. Maria and I also recognized that we had some serious explaining ahead of us, when both Evan and Madison eventually asked critical questions. We knew we would have to share lots of information and details with them, especially about how they became our kids. We had no concerns about doing exactly that.

Since they were toddlers, we talked with Evan and Madison about adoption; what it meant and how it directly related to our family. Obviously, the details we shared with them were age appropriate. We always reinforced that they were both special; were the children God wanted us to love and raise. As little kids, when we asked them if they knew what it meant to be adopted, each would reply, *"I didn't grow in mommy's belly … I grew in her heart!"*

As Evan and Madison got older they realized that they looked different. In fact, when Madison was in second grade, she brought home a family picture she'd drawn. She used brown crayons for Evan and me, and other colors for herself and Maria. On another occasion, the school vice-principal told Maria about an incident one day on the playground. One of Madison's classmates asked her whether Evan was really her brother because they didn't look alike. Madison responded as only a self-confident little girl could. With her hands on her hips she looked at the boy and told him, *"I'm adopted and yes he is my brother!"* The vice-principal told us Madison spoke to the boy in a tone which conveyed he should have had sense enough to figure this out for himself. Yep … that's our little girl!

Fortunately, as Evan and Madison grew up—much more than when I was a kid forty years ago—society is more accepting of families like mine. Mixed-race couples and blended families have become commonplace. Movies and TV programs commonly depict mixed-race families, blended families, families composed of kids with different last names, and families with step-children. Equally common are families formed through adoption. It's quite a different time from when I was a kid. I appreciated this societal progress even more, while sorting through my parent's belongings after they passed away. Let me explain why.

CHAPTER 13

The Picture in the Box

"I have an irrepressible desire to live till I can be assured
that the world is a little better for my having lived in it ."

~ Abraham Lincoln

My experience in looking through my parent's documents was historic, emotional, and personally significant. I'd collected all of their personal papers and documents, which they'd kept in their home and bank safe deposit box. In total, I had six banker's boxes filled with their papers, files, folders, and family photos. I planned to mail them home and then take my time to sort through them. I was staying at the childhood home of my high school best friend's (Peter Gatto) parents. Robert and Connie Gatto were like my *second set of parents*, because I spent so much time at their house throughout high school. We stayed in touch over the years. They insisted that I stay while dealing with my father's funeral arrangements and all the other matters I had to do. The night after my dad's funeral and before flying back to Atlanta, I decided to look through one of the boxes.

As I shuffled through the papers one caught my eye. It looked very familiar and appeared to be an official document. As I focused my eyes on it, I instantly realized that it was an adoption certificate. I looked at it even more closely to make certain of what was in my hands. The piece of paper had my name on it. At that instant, as a middle-aged man, I'd discovered I was adopted—just like my own children. All kinds of emotions flashed through my mind. I was stunned and had lots of questions. Why didn't my parents tell me I was adopted? Who were my birth parents? What was the situation? How did this happen? How old was I when I was adopted? After taking a few minutes to gather my thoughts, I took several deep breaths, re-read my adoption certificate, and came to the best rational conclusion I could. My military background in calmly dealing with stressful situations certainly came in handy right then. I concluded that like my own children's adoption, it must have been the best situation for everyone involved at the time. Calm thinking also helped me understand other discoveries in the box.

After reading a few more papers, some letters, and looking at several photos, I discovered that my mother was my biological mother. But my father was not my biological father. One of the pictures in the box was of a man I believe was my biological father. On wobbly legs, because of the impact of all I had just learned, I walked to the bathroom to look in the mirror. I looked at the face of the man in the photo and then at myself. I did this several times, trying to find any kind of resemblance. Did we have the same shaped nose, or similar skin complexion and body size? Were our eyes and the shape of our ears the same? I returned to the box and looked for more new discoveries. I soon found papers which proved my brother was also adopted. In fact, his biological father was not my biological father. I also found pictures of the man I believe was his biological father. My brother and I were half-brothers.

Having to deal with these *family secrets*, especially in such a short period of time—and on the night after my dad's funeral—was quite a blow for me. Fortunately, I was strong enough to handle the shock of it all and in the home of close and supportive friends. Not to be overwhelmed with further discoveries, I waited to sort through the other boxes of documents and photos when I got back home. But I did think to myself, "*Okay—great! I sure wish I had known all of this a long time ago*". The reality was I didn't know about any of it, and my parents were not around to explain it to me. I had to literally put two-and-two together myself and try my best to figure things out.

I'm confident that if my parents were still alive—and I had the opportunity to ask them about all of this information—we would have had long and in-depth conversations. I had to be satisfied that we would someday have that conversation when we meet again in Heaven. My more immediate issue was to share all I'd learned with Maria. We would both have to digest this information, and then decide how and when we would eventually share all of this with Evan and Madison. We were already preparing for the inevitable serious questions about their adoptions, birth parents, siblings, and numerous other questions. Now we also had *family secrets* to share with them someday. Our approach would be quite different from my parents. Maria and I agreed not to keep family secrets from them.

Maria and I knew that there will come a time when Evan and Madison will want to know more details about their respective birth families. As they grew up, Evan and Madison were told that they were adopted, that God chose us to be their mom and dad, and other age-appropriate family details. They knew that they were born from different mothers. Through the adoption process we learned information we'll eventually share with them. Evan had older siblings. Recall, this was one of the reasons why

Evan's birth mother gave him up for adoption. She literally told the nurses *"we can't afford another baby"*. So I thank God that she carried Evan to full term and made it to the hospital where Maria worked that day. Madison's birth mother was a high school teen and somehow hid the pregnancy from her family. She put both herself and her baby at great risk by having the delivery at home. Madison's birth father skipped town. Also, because Madison's birth parents were so young, she may now have half-brothers or half-sisters. Again, I can only thank God that we were again in the right place and at the right time to adopt Madison.

After their adoptions were complete, each of the files for Evan and Madison were several inches thick. They contain information gathered by our adoption attorney, including medical records, brief family medical histories, family names and ages, and numerous preliminary and final adoption documents. Maria and I have had no contact with any of the birth parents since the adoptions. But if asked, Maria and I would openly and willingly share and explain the files with Evan and Madison. Also, if either Evan or Madison were to ask us to help track down their biological parents or siblings, we would do everything we could to help them connect with their birth families.

Maria and I hope that both Evan and Madison will always recognize us as their parents. We've often watched movies, documentaries or TV programs dealing with adoption. From those sources, we've learned adopted girls, more often than adopted boys, have a greater desire to know about their biological family. Madison might want to know details about her birth mother; what she looked like, her height, her hair or eye color, or whether she had other children. Madison may want to know about why her birth father abandoned her. Equally important, Evan might want details about his birth family. He may want to meet his birth parents or get to know his siblings. If asked, Maria and I will not hesitate to help Evan and Madison find answers to those and many other questions.

That said, it begs the question—why didn't my parents have the same perspective with me? That's a question I can't answer. Yet, I've concluded I don't think any less of my mom and dad because they didn't tell me I was adopted. I was a grown man with my own family before discovering this fact. Candidly, I have no desire to track down my biological father after so many years—assuming that he is still alive. Even if I could find him, what would I ask? And what would the answers prove? Instead of getting answers, it would probably only raise many more questions, bring up long forgotten memories or potentially uncover painful emotions. Imagine if I walked into his family's life so many years later? I can't and won't do it.

The man who raised me was my dad. He taught me how to ride a bike and throw a baseball. He spanked me when I took the *batcha* from my mom, scolded me when I ran away from home, and was disappointed when I got drunk as a teen. He also taught me right from wrong, supported me when I didn't understand why strangers called me terrible names. He modeled for me that my self-esteem did not depend on the acceptance of others, especially ignorant people. For only a few short moments— after I saw my biological father's picture and read his letters my mother kept hidden in her personal papers—did I have any desire to meet him. He had written my mother when I was a baby and wanted to know how she and I were doing. As far as I know, this was all the contact he had with my mom and me. Though my birth father was the biological reason I am here, he didn't raise me. My dad did!

It's amazing how the process of adopting my children actually helped me with my own perspective on being adopted myself.

Initially, it was a shock. But, what I'd learned in the process of adopting Evan and Madison made the realization of my own adoption less traumatic. Birth parents give up their children for adoption for any number of reasons. We knew Evan's birth parents simply couldn't afford to raise another baby. But they loved him and took him to full term. Madison's birth mother was probably too young to raise a baby, but she also carried her to full term and was willing to let her be adopted. I'm confident both sets of birth parents loved their babies, even if they couldn't raise them. I will assume my birth father loved me, and for reasons I may never know, he couldn't stay with my mom to help raise me. Maria and I love Evan and Madison unconditionally. We love them regardless of how they came into our lives, and we know that God caused it to happen. It's all about the love we have for our children and the love my parents had for me.

Certainly, the time when I grew up in the 1960s and 70s was quite different than when my kids grew up. What is constant and consistent during both timeframes, is the love parents have for their children. Parents will do whatever is necessary for the benefit of their kids: how they raise them, provide for them, keep them safe and support them. Most parents probably want their kids to have a better life than they had. Clearly, my parents did the best they could to shelter me from other peoples' harsh words, finger points, and ignorance. They strengthened me to eventually handle my own challenges after I left home. My parents faced many uncomfortable circumstances in their lives. Their marriage as a mixed-race couple was against the acceptable norms at the time. I'm sure they had fear and trepidation about the issues they would have to deal with. They needed the U.S. Army's permission to marry and married in a neutral country to avoid violating America's laws. They didn't know what would happen when they returned during America's turbulent Civil Rights Movement. Would they get arrested? Would their marriage still be recognized? What would be the reaction when they went to public places? Would some people even want to harm them? Growing up they demonstrated confidence and courage to overcome life's hurdles and challenges. They modeled for me their love, joy, peace, patience, kindness, goodness, faithfulness, gentleness, and self-control. They endured against the odds. They instilled pearls of wisdom into me, so I would be able to handle my own challenges, regardless of whatever fork in the road I chose to travel down. At the time when my parents married as a bi-racial couple, society could not see their value, just their skin color. During my childhood, I was too young to always understand or fully appreciate them. By sorting through their keepsakes, documents, and photos, I saw how they significantly impacted me in dramatic ways. Maria and I now had to do the same; to encourage and support Evan and Madison.

CHAPTER 14

Nothing Is As Constant As Change

"Nothing is really ours until we share it."

~ C.S. Lewis

A popular saying is, *"nothing is as constant as change"*. As a grown adult, while emptying my childhood home following my parent's death, I discovered keepsakes, photos, and documents that shocked me to my core. As a husband, father, and businessman, I had to deal with long hidden secrets. I certainly didn't expect to discover what was among my parent's files and personal papers. But, I had no control

Dad with his grand babies; Evan and Madison

over the situation. I certainly would have preferred knowing this information directly from my parents. But they hadn't shared this information with me while I grew up and were no longer alive. Interestingly, shortly before my father passed away I may have had the opportunity of learning about some of those family secrets.

Not long after my mom died, Maria and I seriously considered having my dad live with us. Over several trips to visit him in California we realized his health was deteriorating. We invited him to spend time with us in Georgia so we could look after him, and he could also know Evan and Madison better. We were willing to turn our bonus room into his bedroom or convert our unfinished basement into a fully functional living space for him. Atlanta had a Veterans Administration (VA) hospital where he could get much needed and deserved care. There were grocery stores, restaurants, and a large shopping mall only a few miles from our home. We also had military bases in Marietta and in downtown Atlanta. After much prodding from us, he agreed to a short visit to give it a try. I arranged for his flight and had a cousin in Richmond drive him to the San Francisco airport. I met him when he landed at Atlanta's Hartsfield-Jackson airport.

I was thrilled to see him when he was assisted off the flight in a wheelchair. He seemed equally happy to see us and looked forward to his visit. He played with and fed Evan and Madison, even getting on the floor with them. We drove him around Atlanta, took him to our church and got him comfortable with the area. We also took him to the VA Hospital, the local mall, and several Atlanta attractions including the King Center. He'd always wanted to visit Dr. Martin Luther King's childhood home, crypt, and the Ebenezer Baptist Church where Dr. King and his father preached.

Dad visits Rev. Dr. MLK Jr. crypt and the King Center in Atlanta, GA

Unfortunately, at the end of the week, he told us that he wanted to go back to his California home. His stay with us was short. It wasn't that he didn't enjoy his time with us, just that he was too accustomed to his own surroundings. He missed his friends, shops, restaurants, and routine. He wanted to go back to Richmond. Even after Maria and I had a long conversation with him to discuss all of the reasons why he should stay with us, we couldn't convince him. We practically begged him to stay, but it didn't work. With tears in his eyes he told us he wanted to go back home. It was a very sad day when I drove him to the Atlanta airport for his return flight to the other side of the country.

Afterward, we all often talked to him on the phone. Evan and Madison clamored to speak their toddler-talk with their grandpa. I flew out to visit him a few more times. But with each phone call and visit, I could tell that his health was getting worse. In fact, I took a call late one night from one of his doctors. She told me that his diabetes had seriously affected the blood circulation in one of his legs. She couldn't save it and I gave her permission to amputate it. A few months later, I realized that dementia had advanced to the point where it was taking his memory. During several of our phone calls, I knew he didn't know who I was anymore. Our conversations were short and it seemed like I was talking to a stranger rather than to my dad. But, I was always happy just to hear his voice. At the end of each call, I made sure I told him I loved him. I didn't know if that call might have been our last conversation. His health had gotten so bad I had to put him in a convalescent home and flew out to see him. At the end of my visit, I gave him a hug and kiss, even though he didn't recognize me. After I left his room, I cried uncontrollably in my rental car in the parking lot. I know this was the last time I would see my dad alive. A few days later, I got a call in the middle of the night from one of my cousins. My dad had died. The combination of his many illnesses and a heart attack took his life. He was now with my mother again. He was also with his parents who he hadn't seen since his own childhood. My dad was in a better place. He wasn't in pain anymore. My brother and I made the final arrangements so he was buried in the same plot with our mom. We coordinated to give him a funeral with military honors. Tears rolled down my cheeks as taps was played for him at the end of the graveside ceremony. My brother kept the folded American flag presented to us by the uniformed U. S. Army soldiers. One of them said the following words that were so appropriate for our dad:

On behalf of the President of the United States, the United States Army and a grateful nation, please accept this flag as a symbol of appreciation for your loved one's honorable and faithful service.

After my dad's funeral, I reflected on how my parents had impacted me and imparted so much on my life. I was born during a unique time and into a unique situation. My mother was one race and my father was another. As a child of mixed-race parents and during a traumatic time in America's Civil Rights history, my childhood was filled with being called rude names, epithets, pointed at, told I wasn't black enough, and experiencing many other humiliating issues directed at me by ignorant people. I moved a lot and adapted to new places. In school I had lots of temptations but avoided them. I had the knack of making friends easily and adjusting to whatever circumstances in which I found myself, because of the foundational *courageous confidence* my parents modeled for me. All of this helped me get through high school, get accepted into and graduate from West Point, become a successful U.S. Army Infantry and Green Beret Officer, and achieve success in all of my civilian jobs. Most importantly, it continues to help me as a husband to Maria and father to Evan and Madison.

The Williams Family on a family vacation in Florida

It has been critical to how I've managed the bumps and ruts I've encountered along life's path. I want my story to encourage you to not let roadblocks, hurdles, ignorant people, even situations that seem overwhelming, to keep you down. Through the experiences of my childhood, my military and civilian careers, the death of my parents, my marriage to Maria, and the adoption of Evan and Madison, I've developed a simple philosophy to better understand the impact that all of these events have had on me:

Things happen ... things change ... and then more things happen. Some things are expected and others are not. Deal with it! Have faith that there is a reason for everything. Trust God to get through it all. We may not know or even understand those reasons at the time. God will reveal His reasons on His agenda.

Growing up I encountered people who did not consider me worthy of association. For others, I was the target of their rude comments and taunts. As a child, I continuously saw my parents model how to handle those situations, especially when people acted as if their mental and verbal punishment brought some sort of justice. Similarly, my response toward people who've offended me was to display the character that my parents taught me. Maria and I model this same perspective for Evan and Madison. We have taught them not to respond to evil with evil, rudeness with rudeness, or stupidity with stupidity. Frankly, where societal norms would dictate an eye for an eye or tooth for a tooth response, I consider those pitiful human tendencies. No one who plays by those rules stands out from the crowd. Don't let offenses—large and small, real and imagined—rob us of the joy we are entitled to have. Only with God's grace can we all overcome life's challenges and obstacles.

I'm thankful that the harsh words, taunts, and rudeness that I experienced as a kid are not as common today. That said, there are still ignorant people around. As I finished this book in the summer of 2013, there were recent national news stories demonstrating how some people continue to act rude and nasty. Several people left terrible *anonymous* Facebook comments about a General Mills Cheerios® commercial which featured an adorable mixed-race little girl, her white mom and black dad. The commercial starts with a curly-haired cutie talking to her mom, about the benefits of eating Cheerios. *"Dad told me that Cheerios is good for your heart. Is that true?"* she asks. After her mother agrees, the little girl runs off. Then you see her dad waking up from a nap on the sofa, with his chest covered in Cheerios. Somehow this ad, which ends in love, has generated a lot of hate from some ignorant people. In fact, because the hateful comments against the bi-racial family got so bad, General Mills was forced to disable the comments feature of their Facebook and YouTube sites.[16]

Another situation which made national news occurred at the third game of the 2013 NBA Finals between the San Antonio Spurs and Miami Heat. An eleven year old Mexican-American boy, Sebastien De La Cruz, sang the National Anthem. Several people made numerous racist and unbelievably ugly comments on twitter, such as:

Who dat lil Wetback sangin the national anthem at the #Heat game????"
"9 out of 10 chance that kid singing the national anthem is illegal."
"Is this the American National Anthem or the Mexican Hat Dance? Get this lil kid out of here."
"One of the Three Amigas child singing the National Anthem"
"You really had a Mexican sing the national anthem? Go to hell San Antonio."

Fortunately, those negative comments were countered by several positive comments such as,

"The kid was fantastic, a few minutes before tip-off, he walked out onto the court in full mariachi get-up and sang 'The Star-Spangled Banner' with so much strength that you could fully believe in the American dream."

"The kid was dynamic. He was theatrical as it gets. He hit all the high notes. He stayed long on the low notes."

Sebastien and his family live in San Antonio. He heard about the Twitter attacks. But the fifth-grader took a mature-beyond-his-age high road. On his own Twitter account, he wrote: *"Please do not pay attention to the negative people. I am an American living the American Dream. This is part of the American life."* Even San Antonio's mayor, Julian Castro, was one of hundreds of people who offered the boy words of support, writing on his Facebook page: *"Don't let a few negative voices get you down. You are a true talent and you represent the best of our nation's future!"* In an interview, Sebastien said that people don't know his life. *"My father was actually in the U.S. Navy for a pretty long time, and I actually salute him today for that and I just wanna thank him,"* he said. *"People don't know, they just assume that I'm just a Mexican. But I'm not from Mexico, I'm from San Antonio born and raised, true San Antonio Spurs fan."*[17]

While writing this book, another event demonstrated societal change. The celebrity and Southern Chef, Paula Deen, was cited

186

in a recent lawsuit for using the N-word and creating demeaning work conditions against Black co-workers in her restaurants. As a result of this lawsuit, corporations that helped create Deen's $60 million empire—such as Smithfield Hams, Walmart, Target, Home Depot and Caesar's Entertainment—have dropped their endorsements of her like a hot potato, now that she has been exposed. Also, the Food Network will not renew her contract. Paula Deen now faces numerous challenges because of her accused "violent, sexist and racist behavior". [18]

Though these examples demonstrate how some positive societal changes have happened, others have not. The term *twitter thugs* has evolved to describe those who use the modern technology of twitter to anonymously advance their ignorance and caustic opinions. Only a generation ago vicious racists hid behind hoods and robes. Others used the darkness of night to conduct their evil. Still others used their police authority, high pressure water hoses, billy clubs, attack dogs, or church bombings to demonstrate their vengeance. Now some ignorant people use social media as a tool to advance their racism and hatred.

America has made tremendous strides toward racial equality. More elected officials than ever before are Black. State governors and other civil servants in all levels of leadership positions nationwide are African-American. Many Fortune 500 CEO's, University Chancellors and Presidents, Generals and Admirals throughout the military are Black. The President, a mixed-race African-American, is currently serving his second term. Though these are all tremendous accomplishments, America still has more progress to make. *Racial profiling,* the use of race or ethnicity as grounds for suspecting someone of having committed an offense, is on the rise. Several state legislators have imposed unjustified restrictions on who can cast a ballot. These state and local jurisdictions have passed or attempted to pass laws eliminating same day registration, instituted photo ID requirements, shortened hours for registration, and moved polling places in ways that will disadvantage minority communities. It's ironic that these issues still exist while we simultaneously celebrate the fiftieth anniversary of the March on Washington for equality and freedom, Dr. Martin Luther King Jr.'s famous *I Have A Dream* speech, and the Civil Rights movement. As we look back with nostalgia on the way things were and reflect on the enormous strides that have been made in racial justice, we are also confronted with a political culture that seems to have taken a step backwards. That said, I want to be part of the progress and help overcome today's challenges. Rather than remain jaded by my experiences growing up as a mixed-race kid, I've chosen to share my story in hopes that it will encourage others to overcome their challenges. Also, two and a half years ago—after eleven years of experience as a trainer, speaker, and facilitator for two small firms—I decided to start my own company to share critical insights as a motivational and professional speaker.

Eddie sharing some insights at a presentation.
Source: Tom Milesko Photography

My company conducts workshops, presentations, and keynote speeches on a variety of critical topics; time management and productivity, conflict resolution, team-building, emotional intelligence, negotiating, organizational effectiveness, diversity and others. I share insights with business executives, mid-level managers, students, teachers, administrators, government agency employees, sales representatives, and people from all walks of life and all over the country.

Because of the tragedy of September 11, 2001 and my prior military service, I also serve in the Georgia State Defense Force. About twenty-five states have a similar state defense force, state guard or state reserve force. The GSDF is a voluntary military organization that assists the Georgia Army and Air National Guard during state emergency situations such as search & rescue, hurricane evacuation, and medical emergencies. Over the past ten years I've held positions as the Headquarters Recruiting Officer, Public Affairs Officer, Operations Company Commander, Battalion Executive Officer and Commander of 911th Support Battalion. I'm currently the Commander of the 76th Support Brigade at the Clay National Guard Center, Marietta, GA, and hold the rank of Colonel. See http://www.gasdf.com/.

Through my experiences, strengths, talents, and abilities, I daily strive to be the best husband, father, business professional, soldier and leader I can be. I don't claim to know everything, but enjoy sharing what I know and what I've learned. I want to do my part in sharing insights that will help the individuals, families, employees, businesses, and other business owners I encounter.

Maybe my story taught you something about America's Civil Rights history. Maybe it will positively impact relationships between spouses or assist parents to better relate with their children. Maybe my words will allow someone to overcome their own experiences of being bullied or humiliated. I encourage each reader to take away something positive from my story. Do not be satisfied by judging yourself simply by looking at any snapshot of time in your life. It's only one second of years filled with happiness, sadness, pleasure, fulfillment, failure, and achievement. Your self-esteem, success, and satisfaction are not solely dependent on your own efforts, but from the contributions and support of those who continually encouraged you all along the way. The most admired are often the most humble because they live their life to the fullest, not by being boastful about their own efforts. They learn and share their experiences and let their talents take them to places they could not have imagined. Some people have limited vision and don't see things beyond their immediate focus. Do not have that narrow and limiting view. Have a broad and wide perspective in your activities, goals, and plans because of what you've learned through your interests, talents, and abilities. Get out of your comfort zone. Take steps daily to achieve your goals. How you get there may not be down the road you expected to travel. Measure your accomplishments not by status, but by the journey and legacy you create and leave behind. I'm reminded of Civil Rights icon, former Atlanta Mayor and former United Nations Ambassador, Andrew Young's comments, when he so aptly defined the human spirit;

Every day we watch and we're amazed by your generosity, your humanity, your selflessness, and your unwavering capacity for love. We marvel at how you overcome adversity and how you celebrate success. We know it's not always easy. We've seen life throw you some curveballs. And when misfortune, hard times and even tragedy comes around, it's your ability to find hope, regain happiness, and your resolve that inspires us the most. [19]

Sometimes we have to push ourselves beyond our perceived limited abilities or self-imposed boundaries. My parents demonstrated for me how they crossed physical boundaries to get married and shattered societal boundaries throughout their lives together. The next time you feel helpless, hopeless, in an uncomfortable situation, or in over your head, remember those who've faced difficult challenges, overcame them, and thrived. Discover how they did it and use that knowledge to chart your own course. Lose sight of the shore as you focus on and advance toward your own destination in an ocean of opportunity. You can't do the same things you've always done in the same ways you've always done them and expect different results. Be willing to learn along the way. Share what you've learned and experienced—even if it uncovers family secrets.

Madison and Evan

End Notes

1.   *Sticks & Stones Exposed, The Power of Our Words*, by Dave Weber, Self Published, Atlanta, GA 2004. p. 3.

2.   U.S. Army's Chief of Military History, 18 June 1965. http://www.history.army.mil/books/wwii/11-4

3.   *CharlesSwindolquotes*, http://www.goodreads.com/author/quotes/5139.Charles_R_Swindoll

4.   *The 7 Habits of Highly Effective People. Powerful Lessons in Personal Change*, by Stephen R. Covey, Simon & Schuster, New York, 1990. p. 92.

5.   *Start Where You Are*, by Chris Gardner. HarperCollins, 2009. p. 5.

6.   *The 7 Habits of Highly Effective People. Powerful Lessons in Personal Change*, by Stephen R. Cover, Simon & Schuster, New York, 1990. p.92.

7.   Dialogue paraphrased from *Alice's Adventures in Wonderland*, by Lewis Carroll. First published by MacMillan, London, in 1865.

8.   *The Law of Clarity, Brian Tracy's Blog*, Brian Tracy, September 22, 2008. http://www.briantracy.com/blog/leadership-success/the-law-of-clarity

9. *Hank Aaron quotes.* http://africanamericanquotes.org/hank-aaron.html

10. *May 25, 1961 before a joint session of Congress. In this speech, President John F. Kennedy, stated that the United States should achieve a goal by "landing a man on the moon and returning him safely to the earth" by the end of the decade.*

11. *Some of the world's greatest men and women. Unknown author.*

12. *The Greatest Generation,* by Tom Brokaw, Random House, New York, 1998. p. 1.

13. West Point Mission, *http://www.usma.edu/SitePages/Home.aspx*

14. *Charles Darwin quote.* http://www.goodreads.com/quotes/18875-it-is-not-the-strongest-of-the-species-that-survives

15. Iran Hostage Situation 1979. Wikipedia http://en.wikipedia.org/wiki/Ira_hostage_crisis

16. Cheerios commercial with biracial family causes controversy: Company disables comments on YouTube. See YouTube video on: http://youtu.be/kYofm5d5Xdw

17. Mexican-American boy singing National Anthem at NBA finals attacked online http://www.kansascity.com/2013/06/13/4291546/reports-sebastien-de-la-cruz-to.html

18. Paula Deen: A Scarlett O'Hara, corporate-style. Workers World. July 1, 2013. http://www.workers.org/articles/2013/07/01/paula-deen-a-scarlett-ohara-corporate-style/

19. Andrew Young definition of the Human Spirit. http://www.11alive.com/video/2327897758001/1/11Alive-Together-Andrew-Young

NOTE:

Source of photo of SF Soldier on horseback in Afghanistan is commons.wikimedia.org. U.S. Special Forces ride horseback working with members of the Northern Alliance, Operation Enduring Freedom, Afghanistan, 12NOV2001, Photo by Master Sergeant Chris Spence.

Source of photo of Eddie conducting presentation is Tom Mileshko, Tom Mileshko Photography, tom@milepix.com, 404-713-0324.

Special Forces tab, Special Forces crest, Ranger tab, Airborne tab as watermark on back cover are public domain images:

https://www.google.com/search?q=public+domain+images+special+forces&tbm=isch&tbo=u&source=univ&sa=X&ei=6mAWUq-0K6eU2wW2qoCICQ&ved=0CCoQsAQ&biw=1280&bih=595

Appendix #1: Glossary of Common West Point Terms
(Source: http://www.westpoint.edu/admissions/Lists/Glossary %20 of%20Terms/AllItems.aspx)

1	**USMA**	United States Military Academy, also synonymous with West Point
2	**DAD**	Directorate of Admissions or the Admissions Office
3	**ODIA**	Athletics
4	**USMAPS**	United States Military Academy Prep School
5	**WPPSP**	West Point Preparatory School Program
6	**JAG**	Judge Advocate General - the 'law firm' of the Army
7	**Corps of Cadets**	The population of Cadets at West Point
8	**Barracks**	The residence facilities where Cadets live while at West Point
9	**Mess**	The Mess Hall is the facility where cadets eat their meals every day
10	**Beast**	The last week of the 6-week basic training for Cadets
11	**Cadre**	Upper Class cadets orienting new Cadets
12	**Plebe**	Cadets in their 1st year at West Point, similar to being a college freshman
13	**Yucks or Yearlings**	Cadets in their 2nd year at West Point , similar to being a college sophomore
14	**Cows**	Cadets in their 3rd year at West Point, similar to being a college junior
15	**Firstie**	Cadets in their 4th Year at West Point, similar to being a college senior
16	**Sir**	How to address a male officer
17	**Ma'am**	How to address a female officer
18	**Full Bird**	A Colonel in the US Army
19	**Cadet Honor Code**	The pledge that all cadets live by, that a cadet will not lie, cheat, or steal, or tolerate those who do
20	**Candidate**	Someone, typically High school seniors and/or juniors applying for West Point
21	**Candidate Kit**	An online "package" of forms and instructions you need to complete your application
22	**Candidate Portal**	A portal where current candidates can access their application files online, a password-protected site where you find your Candidate Kit
23	**Candidate Questionnaire**	An initial candidate application which is considered "starting a file"

24	**Candidate Statement**	Three questions that the applicant (Candidate) answers in essay form as part of the application package (Candidate Kit)
25	**CFA Candidate Fitness**	Physical assessment that you must pass to be considered for admission to West Point
26	**Corps of Cadets**	The student body at West Point
27	**DoDMERB**	Department of Defense Medical Examination Review Board which schedules the required medical exam prior to acceptance consideration at West Point
28	**Letter of Assurance**	Communication to an applicant (Candidate) that he or she will most likely be offered admission upon completion of their application (Candidate Kit)
29	**Nomination**	A formal recommendation from a Congressional member or other authorized official that is required for admission
30	**Reception Day or R-Day**	The day that the incoming class of cadets reports to West Point, usually the last Monday in June
31	**Parents Almanac**	Helpful information for parents that is posted on the Candidate Portal, usually in February or March
32	**Parents Clubs**	A support network for families of cadets located throughout the U.S.
33	**Personal Data Record**	A basic form that the applicant (Candidate) fills out as part of the application process (Candidate Kit)
34	**Prospectus**	The "viewbook" is available in print and online, it explains requirements and important aspects of a West Point education.
35	**SLS**	Summer Leadership Seminar, a week-long immersion experience for prospective students the summer before their senior year of high school
36	**The Long Gray Line**	The prestigious corps of West Point graduates who represent high achievement and the promise of outstanding, ethical leadership
37	**West Point Field Force**	Active duty, retired Army officers, or civilian members who help recruit future cadets
38	**Cullum Number**	Reference and identification number assigned to each graduate, often referred to as the "C-number"
39	**Thayer Award**	Given annually by the academy since 1958, the award honors an outstanding citizen whose service and accomplishments in the national interest exemplify the academy's motto, "Duty, Honor, Country"

40	Goat Engineer Game	A football game between the "Goats" (the bottom half of the senior (Firstie) class academically), and the "Engineers" (the top half). Held just before the Army-Navy game
41	The Area	Designated area of the cadet barracks courtyard
42	The Howitzer	Annual yearbook
43	Bugle Notes	The "plebe bible"
44	Companies	The groups of cadets that you live with
45	Scrambling	The changing of companies
46	First Captain	Highest ranking Firstie, also known as the Brigade Commander
47	IOCT	Indoor Obstacle Course Test
48	DMI	Department of Military Instruction

Appendix #2: Missions of Special Forces
(Source: http://www.goarmy.com/special-forces/primary-missions.html)

Special Forces Soldiers are either on a real-world mission or training for one. Their missions are conducted worldwide and are sometimes classified. They range from Counterterrorism missions to humanitarian efforts to Unconventional Warfare.

COUNTERTERRORISM

Special Forces are often deployed to preclude, preempt and resolve terrorist incidents abroad. They prevent, deter and respond to terrorist activities and train other nations' military in the basics of fighting terrorism.

DIRECT ACTION

Direct Action missions are short duration strikes that are used when Special Forces want to seize, capture, recover or destroy enemy weapons and information or recover designated personnel or material.

FOREIGN INTERNAL DEFENSE

This mission is used to organize, assist and train the military and national defense forces of foreign governments to protect their citizens from aggressors.

SPECIAL RECONNAISSANCE

These intelligence-gathering activities monitor as much about the enemy's movement and operations as possible.

UNCONVENTIONAL WARFARE

Special Forces have long employed the use of Unconventional Warfare (UW), a.k.a. guerilla warfare, to train, equip, advise and assist forces in enemy-held or controlled territory.

About the author

Eddie Williams is a West Point graduate where he earned a Bachelor of Science degree. He's a U.S. Army veteran and former Airborne, Ranger, and Green Beret. He also holds an MBA from Kennesaw State University's Executive-MBA program.

For over a dozen years, Eddie has been a professional speaker and consultant. As managing partner of E&M Williams Consulting Group, LLC in Atlanta, GA, his firm conducts workshops, presentations, and keynote speeches on such topics as: personal productivity, stress management, emotional intelligence, diversity, conflict resolution, negotiating, team building, self-esteem, and motivation. He, his wife Maria, and their two children, Evan and Madison, live in metro-Atlanta, Georgia.

Clients include: FedEx, Cintas Corporation, Centers for Disease Control and Prevention (CDC), Federal Aviation Administration, AFLAC, The Coca-Cola Company, Deluxe Corporation, Waste Management, MetLife, Mutual of Omaha, IHOP, numerous schools and school systems, and industry specific associations nationwide.

Author Website: www.eddie-williams.com
Author email address: eddiewilliams49@gmail.com
Book website: www.sonofasoldier.us